Cupid's C*ckups

BY
CHELSEA BLACK

First printed in the United Kingdom, 2020

Published by Conscious Dreams Publishing
www.consciousdreamspublishing.com

Edited by Rhoda Molife
www.molahmedia.com

Typeset by Oksana Kosovan

ISBN: 978-1-913674-32-8

Table of Contents

Preface

Hello, my fellow singirls (and to you open minded singuys who care to read too)!

Yes, I knew you wouldn't let me get away without finally resorting to writing a book. But I know what you may be thinking – not another book telling me that I have to love myself before anyone can fall in love with me. No, it really isn't. We all know we need to love ourselves – that's a given – but even when we do it, it doesn't necessarily mean the perfect partner comes along at the right time. Besides, I've read all those books as part of my research and I'm still single.

So, clearly, I'm either not reading them properly or they don't always work. Despite the daily mantras and the rules etc, there is a certain amount of either luck or compromise to being in a great, sustainable, healthy relationship. I'm out of luck and compromise is a colour that clashes with everything I own. If compromise was a colour it would be that awful beige-like mess of shades meshed together that doesn't look good on most people. It's so not my look. So that's my excuse for being single or singirl as I like to call it. Here's to sin and enjoying my singirl-arity.

I'm going to be single until I find somebody that I can be with completely… without compromising to the point of beige. Maybe a strong tan or mahogany. I'm also allergic to forgiving stupidity which makes it hard to get back with some of my exes. I lowkey believe that they're stupid as they let me go. Don't worry, I'm working on this. I'm not working very hard on it as they are *ex* for a reason but I've been told by friends, family and some well-meaning random strangers that I should learn to forgive.

They are all wrong, mind you, because I know that my outlook on life is practically perfect in every way. This is what comes from watching too much *Mary Poppins* as a child. I know what I like and I know how much bullshit I'm willing to tolerate. Turns out it's not very much.

So basically, I'm not here to lecture you. Instead, I'm sharing with you my misadventures and hope that:

1. You recognise the red flags *aka* the 'Danger! Grab your purse and run!' signs ahead of time and avoid the obvious mistakes I made.
2. You recognise a dodgy character and move on if you're still with him because rarely do the bad ones change. It's probably a lost cause. He's not going to grow out of it or evolve no matter how many YouTube motivational videos he watches.
3. You enjoy reading about someone else's misfortunes. Like watching *X-Factor*, it's always those that want to be singers so badly (but no one has told them that they can't sing) that makes for good TV. I reckon it's the same with my dates.

Unlike most, I have had my fair share (and you too I'm sure) of bad dates, disastrous dates and even a few good dates. The good dates would later become reasonably good relationships or dates that I would analyse for days as to why I hadn't heard anything from him, so much so that it made sense to document the disasters for prosperity because when I finally do find a man, I want him to know the *shit* I went through before he came along. And what took him so long? Oh yes, I hate lateness. I strongly believe that he's somewhere south of the river or circling the M25 right now lost and too stubborn to ask for directions.

The format of this book is simple. It's a series of blogs with a little bit more background to each misadventure than you may have read online. It's not always chronological and I'm not going to lie, some of them were just incidents that I didn't learn a thing from. Not every misadventure has a lesson except maybe drink fewer cocktails on a night out and stop making horny decisions. I say incidents as opposed to accidents as I have never tripped and landed on an erect dick. Not every experience is a learning experience surely? Either that or I'm an *extremely* slow learner.

When I was younger, I enjoyed dating, though I did not have the same gusto as those girls who used it to get fed. You know the ones – artists, students and those who feel that their only job in life is to look amazing so that men will treat them with stuff. The modern term is 'rinsers'. I'm not one of them.

When I first started dating again, I assumed it would be over in six months and that I would be safely in another relationship before the end of year. That was 12 years ago. Don't get me wrong my singirls, I love the art and science of dating but there comes a time in our lives when we just don't want to do it anymore. This doesn't mean I hate being a singirl. I just don't want to be single every waking hour of every waking day. There are perfectly good reasons to be in a relationship. Like, who is going to fix stuff? COVID-19 has highlighted my lack of DIY skills and inability to assemble gym equipment. I'm tired of paying for handymen to do the things my nails won't allow me to do. And why don't they clean up after themselves? For the amount they charge... but I digress.

I know there are a lot of books out there about dating: *The Dos & Don'ts, The Best Ways to Get a Man in 30 Days*, or my personal favourites (usually written by guys) the *Mr He Will Marry You IF You Give up Your Whole Identity or Why Being a Bitch is The Way Forward*. I can't claim to be an expert on dating despite my commitment to the hobby. Some of you may question why I keep dating but sadly I'm a victim of an optimistic nature and I assume that nobody can be that terrible. I'm quite often proven wrong. Besides, I have a nagging black family who insist my life is still theirs until I have reproduced. And even then, it will still be theirs. I don't see what I get out of this deal ... I may have to rethink my life's philosophy.

My purpose is a simple and selfish one. I don't want to die alone. I too want to have a partner and children to boss / emotionally manipulate someday and I want the company of another. I want to love and be loved. This doesn't mean that I see every relationship as an opportunity to breed, mind you. Some genetic combinations are best left untested. If you choose to see this book as the bitter ramblings of a single woman feel free. Just make sure you paid for it 'cos this woman may as well get paid if she's forever going to be a bridesmaid. These destination weddings you all insist upon aren't cheap!

Enjoy, my singirls and please leave comments:
- on my blog – *www.chelsea-black.com*
- on the usual social medias – *@chelseablack / @chelseablackuk*

Smooches,
Chelsea Black 2020
xxx

Glossary

BS	Bullshit
DHL	Daddy/Homie/Lover
FB	Fuck Buddy
FuHu	Future Husband
FuBo	Future Boyfriend
LEE	Lucky Effing Escape
Maxine Saj	My buddha belly and permanent nemesis who craves Haribos and chocolates. I'm just here to provide them
ONS	One Night Stand
PoF	Plenty of Fish
Po Po	police
Prick Headfuck	the name for all exes in my phone who I never want to speak to again
Stella	taken from the book and film *How Stella Got Her Groove Back* and referring to a post marriage dating come back
Singirls	the readers who are an army of single women enjoying singirl-arity – being happily single whilst dating
Singletini	single and martini; fabulous and happy whilst being single
SLS	Shag/Long-term partner/Sperm donor. A modern-day alternative to the DHL

PART 1

Dating Ready

1. The Intro

So where did it all begin? Duh… at the beginning of course! Or in my case, the end. Life normally doesn't have an easy beginning but for me, I took the end of a marriage and my introduction back into dating as the start of my misadventures. I've decided to ignore the dating period prior to my reaching 21 as basic training camp and nothing of real consequence. You know there is only so much I can learn from the era where I lived with my parents and disappeared off into London to shop with boys on Oxford Street. Ah yes, the golden days before men revealed that they hated to shop. That only came later. So yes, the beginning.

Once Upon a Time

…there was a twenty-something-year-old princess who lived in a shoebox. Brexit had yet to descend like a fog over London and property prices weren't swirling out of control. Then again everyone lived in a shoe box or a house full of other people's shoes.

She hadn't always lived in a shoebox. Oh no my singirls, her previous abode had been a three bedroomed end of terrace castle in leafier Ealing with her then prince. A sweet man, they had decided that happily ever after wasn't to be their ending and he had banished her from the Ealing castle to the dungeon of a shoebox. Sweet, yes, but charming he clearly was not. A Gemini.

So, swearing never to love again, she took all her belongings (including a multitude of smaller boxes) to live in her shoebox dungeon in Chelsea. At first, she was happy and enjoyed life outside of the castle. Cocktails and chocolate became her constant companions. She joined a band of merry Singletinis and often, though ill-advisedly, she experimented with fancy dress and karaoke.

Despite enjoying her new life, she realised that her time in the dungeon could be better utilised if she actually tried to find a new prince. Not that every princess needed a prince but with a penchant for romantic comedies and an unfavourable economic climate it made both emotional and fiscal sense. She was over any resentment for the first prince and wanted to make mini princes and princesses of her own.

So, where to start? In her early twenties there were wannabe princes everywhere battling for her student hand but as she tentatively got older, she noticed that fewer princes seemed to be around. Where had they all fled? Surely, she wouldn't have to move back to the suburbs to find him. Black cabs rarely went there, and she did love black cabs.

One day, on a rare trip back to Ealing, she stumbled across a psychic at a fair. She asked about her love life and the psychic said she couldn't see anything in the cards. She asked again and the psychic looked confused and said that nothing was coming up. The princess was flummoxed. The psychic told her, "Go and seek it and take note of all that is around you." Confused and disappointed the princess returned to the dungeon to reflect. And then it hit her. Maybe her prince couldn't find her! Maybe he wasn't very partial to the District Line, something she could sympathise with entirely. Or maybe he was just running on African time, because in her mind princes only came from Africa. Way too many Coming to America watching nights in peut-être?

So, she decided to be brave. Why couldn't she be the one to go out there and slay tube delays for her happily ever after? She was a romantic feminist princess after all (DIY and vermin extermination excluded).

And thus began the princess' adventures. She started status updating about her misfortunes and was asked for more. Ah! Perhaps the psychic had meant that she take actual notes? So, she started a column and then a blog. She bought a six-month internet dating subscription, confident that in that time she would find a prince with charm. That was (cough) some years ago and her subscription has since lapsed.

That princess is me, my singirls. My name is Chelsea Black and welcome to my misadventures. Maybe, just maybe, you'll find tales in here that will help you with your own happily-ever-after (prince not supplied but I can tell you how many batteries you may need).

About Me

Ah yes, the 'About Me' section. Normally I love talking about me because it's the one subject I know a lot about. You know when you turn up to those business networking do da things and they tell you that everyone is going to have to do a 60-second pitch? You're standing there thinking to yourself, "F**k! I've got half of a business idea because I hate my boss, my deodorant stopped working around noon and there are no canapés at this thing. I should have stopped off at that last McDonalds."

Well that's how I feel about writing about dating. It's half an idea based on a series of status updates on a certain social network and 500 blogs but, hopefully, by the end of this you'll get the idea that dating in modern times has its challenges. Dating is a minefield of missed opportunities, timewasters and in my case way too much vodka. Vodka has been my friend and oftentimes the enemy that has made me think that a guy was a safer gamble than all the evidence suggested.

Deadlines and word counts – my parents would be so proud. I think they may still be telling people that I'm a journalist, bless them. I guess you could call what I do "life journalism or 'sexual-social anthropology'. Take your pick. Not that they'll see this. I mean, who wants to be confronted with the fact that your daughter is a dating disaster who spends way too much daytime in the local park? A daughter who thinks that the recommended drinking limit for women is 21 units. To be clear, it's 14 units for those of you who also thought that 21 was the right answer (21 is for a man). Oh, and the sex! No one wants to admit that their precious child is out there exploring. Not as much as she would like to mind you but exploring none the less. Sex is sometimes a precursor to the date. Don't judge my singirls, we live in modern times and sometimes you know that it won't be anything more than physical.

Despite loving to think that I'm spontaneous and just flow where life takes me, I'm a girl with a plan. I plan to have babies, get married four times (one down only three more to go!) and am destined for great things. Unfortunately, I'm also severely allergic to crying kids, fall in and out of lust way too quickly and lack the focus for success. But none of this stops me from dreaming. You've got to have dreams, right? I work for myself as an administrator and social group organiser (see reference to park above) but am a full-time virtual bar fly. I'm always on Facebook and Twitter chatting and telling people off for comments that don't make sense or offend my black feminist sensibilities. But, back to the plan. Let's start with the marriages. My four marriages are planned out as thus:

18

1. Starter Husband – the one who seemed like a safe bet in my 20s and a great friend but not the love of my life. At some point in our 20s, all our friends are getting married. Many of us turn to the one that we're dating and think, he's not so bad and he lets me have the last chocolate, so why not? He's the one that will teach you about the legalities of marriage and divorce. Pay attention my singirls. Chances are you'll find him dipping into all sorts of chocolate behind your back and lying about it. But it's a start.

2. Daddy/Homie/Lover or the DHL Husband – the one who will be my one true love and breed with me. He will probably leave me when he wins the lottery and run off with Little Miss New Boobs. Please, universe, don't let him be so clichéd as to run away with his secretary, dental hygienist or the *au pair* (the last one will never happen as I plan to hire lesbians who are 50+ only. If anyone is at risk of running away with the *au pair*, rather it be me).

3. The Stella Husband – the one who will give me back my sexual confidence after the betrayal of what I thought was my one true love, DHL, disappeared with the lottery money and the floozy now only ever referred to as Little Miss New Boobs because the first thing he will do is buy her a decent pair. Sadly, Stella Husband may not be the one as he is likely to only want me for the sex. But I will be generous in giving him some. Bring it on!

4. Care Home Husband – I don't think I need to explain but if my kids go against my rules and put me in a care home then I'm not going in there alone. This one needs to be good at dominos and seducing the remote control off the other old ladies. He also needs to be able to tell amazingly erotic stories as chances are in our 90s, we will not be getting up to as much mischief as I would like. Three times a week will suffice. Hmm unless he's 20 years younger?

I'm happy to combine 2, 3 and 4 into one who will be known as FuHu – Future Husband – for the purposes of this search. He is preceded by FuBo – Future Boyfriend. I suspect there will be more than one FuBo.

As for the children, I have their names, gender and careers all picked out. Yes, yes, I know that they may come along and thwart me with their individuality and surprise me by not being truly amazing at sport, drama and academics but you must have goals, right? To my four yet to be conceived children – sometimes you will hate me but you will learn that I do all that I do for you so that I can have major bragging rights whenever I am around my peers, family or strangers whose children will not be as accomplished. Don't let me down. It's the parental way.

So, more about me just to set the scene. I'm over 21. I'm at the age where men ask me how many kids I've got as opposed to do I have any. Then again this could be due to my permanent buddha belly that I call Maxine Saj. She goes everywhere with me and constantly craves chocolates, champagne, carbs and Woo Woo cocktails. I don't question these desires, I just provide. C is not just for Chelsea as you can see. I love foods started with C too. I have also developed an unhealthy obsession with chewy sweets. They have become my emotional go to if there is no chocolate around. Oh, did I mention I'm lactose intolerant? Yes, sometimes I just have to say no to chocolate which is sad because it's like saying no to a lover… a good lover. Just isn't something you want to do.

My body is of one of the typical Southern or Eastern African designs. Small waist, big hips and a butt. This sadly is not who fashion designers target so I'm always trying to squeeze my assets into ill-fitting clothes. I'm in somewhat of a size denial and refuse to buy anything bigger than a 12. I'm also on perpetual diets which last until I pass a pack of sweets, a bottle of champagne or… chocolate. Not the good chocolate mind, although I don't say no to some Lindor red balls. No, the sort of chocolate that you find squashed at the bottom of kid's school satchels. I'm addicted to cheap chocolate. Twix and Twirl. Lion Bar and Galaxy if you're buying.

I call everyone by the same few pet names. This is because I meet so many people that I can't be bothered to remember them all. This has been made worse by Twitter. I can't remember real names or Twitter names either. So, if I call you my singirls, lovely, sweetie, darling, babes, dear, pookie or boo then know that it's all love.

I also find this much easier since I started dating. These random dates and ONS – One Night Stands – want to be individualized and called by their name at all times. But no, easier not to until they've proven themselves worthy of a name. I also change all exes' names that I don't want to speak to in my phone to Prick Headfuck or Loser Do Not Answer. This however got complicated as I didn't know which Prick or Loser to be angry at for pestering me and it isn't fair to assume that it was one of the other Pricks or Losers was it?

I drink, don't drive and date quite a bit. Some may say that I'm demanding, others, that I'm not demanding enough. I've put up with some pretty awful dates as you will read over the next few chapters. I don't really do things like cook and clean to prove to men how domesticated I am. Don't get me wrong I know how to do both, but I choose not to as a feminist stance against the man... that's my excuse and I'm sticking to it. Mama Black would probably like it to be added that she did teach me to do both, bless her. I'm just a domestic rebel.

I live in London and will not be removed unless under the influence of lots of champagne and a Tiffany ring. In fact, I saw the perfect champagne pink bauble ring in their window the other day. I think the ring, a house in Zone 1, a great credit rating to counterbalance mine *and* patience makes for the perfect compromise for being stuck in a relationship. Oh, and a credit card with no limit would be yummy but I'm a realist. You can't have it all. Just a black Amex will do.

Now I would love to stop and chat some more about me, but you've just reminded me that I need to contrive a subtle way for my latest lust bunny to see the bauble ring. It's been three weeks and I'm hopeful. So what if he hasn't called me for a week. A girl with a plan, that's me.

Please note that nearly all the men in these books have had their names changed to protect them from abuse and harassment. Abuse and harassment from me. I do recognize that they are not necessarily bad people – they may have just not been particularly nice to me on the day of our date or afterwards. Some of them are just opportunists who prey on the weak and vulnerable (that's me by the way and all the other women who are told that they will be called and never, ever are) and see the whole dating thing as a game. But I'm not really bitter. I'm just setting my record straight. Some men are just up to nonsense and I have all your names. Well, your screen names at least Sir Tongue-a-lot. You've been warned!

I'm left-handed in a right-handed world. I refuse to do anything sensible with my hair or clothes. I'm allergic to office politics and I have a note from my doctor who also happens to be a relative. Anything I do can always seem like more of a challenge but I never imagined that dating after marriage was going to be this bloody hard. I'm not going to lie to you my singirls, I've enjoyed most of it and some of it has been educational. But the reality is that my journey is one of finding alternatives to the happily ever after. The happily ever after that involves tricking a man into marrying me. Oh, don't get me wrong. That happily ever after is still an option but it's not the only option we have as single ladies. And not every man is marriage material, right? Some are strictly there for a night or a winter.

I'm also not a victim. Divorce is rarely one person's fault although in this case I do believe it was nearly all his fault. I think before men propose to women they should go through a course with a proposal and commitment specialist who will assess their relationship readiness. I would run this course myself, but I know that I'd get too annoyed by their 'Bambi-learning-to-walk-stumbling-through-their-thoughts' behaviour.

Mine made all the right noises but he wasn't ready and definitely not ready for me. I accept that not all relationships will work out no matter how much work one puts into them, so instead you pack up the Mini Cooper and move to a shoe box. Well, I can't drive so he kept Ronnie, the Mini Cooper. I miss her. We had some great adventures together.

This seems important now as recently I have deleted Facebook from my dating options after an unfortunate incident with a so-called fan who turned out to be a waste of time. But more on that in book two, *Dating Recession*. What I'm going to do now is talk about the many stages of dating from 'divorced reality' to 'dating readiness'. That's the period after a relationship where you learn to let go of all your dating expectations for the reality of what's happening out there in the dating world. Not an easy concept you understand and one that took me three years to grasp. What can I tell you – I'm a very slow learner.

But first let's look at the discrimination that us single women are subjected to, then we'll get back to dating and my search for that happily ever after.

The Divorce Phenomenon

So, there is a strange post-divorce phenomenon that occurs that I don't quite understand. It's the response to telling people that you're divorced. When men declare themselves as such, they usually get told that they must have had a lucky escape and that there are plenty more women out there. When women say it, people look upon them with pity and ask stupid questions based on their inability to conceive that any woman would be happy that she was in fact divorced. The first thing people do is ask what went wrong.

When someone tells me that they're getting married, I may be interested enough to ask them about the proposal and their upcoming wedding plans because I'm polite but I'm never going to ask someone why! It's the weirdest thing. No one asked me why I got married until I got divorced at which point my private life became open for discussion. Or maybe I should ask friends and strangers why they are getting married. Maybe I should scream, "OMG are you pregnant?" "Is he old and only now realising that he can't do better?" "Are you settling because you're in your 40s?" (The answer to these questions sadly, are usually yes so, tread carefully. You may lose friends and acquaintances).

One guy asked me if I felt like a failure. I asked him why and he said, "Well, you obviously couldn't make your marriage work so I guess you would feel like a failure." He had various kids scattered across the UK so I could see how his inability to commit to anything longer than a shag would make him an expert. But his response was telling. A marriage failing is the woman's fault apparently.

So yes, next time you come across your newly divorced friend spare them the inquisition. Chances are they've heard it before and what they really want to know is… where are all the cute guys. Your girl needs some Stella! Not the drink but the young-bodied-in-the-sun sex kind from *How Stella Got Her Groove Back*.

Question 1. The big question: OMG what happened? What went wrong?

This is the most insensitive question out there. If you tell me that your relative died, I don't ask for an autopsy report. No, I say I'm sorry for your loss and I move on. Divorce is the death of a marriage and yet everyone swoops on it like vultures picking at bones. I don't think any divorce is that straightforward. Even if one or both of you cheated that is unlikely to be the sole reason the marriage ended.

Few come out of a divorce lightly. I told my one friend's mum that I was divorcing, and she shouted, "Mazel tov!" then gave me a great big hug. She had been married three times and knew that a divorce is not as straightforward as just feeling bad about it ending. There is some relief to something that was no longer making you happy finally being over.

Question 2. Deciphering how evil you are: Were there kids involved? Was there anyone else involved?

If you say that yes you have kids, they look at you with even more sadness. So, not only were you a horrendous wife but also a bad mother because you couldn't keep your family unit together. Divorce isn't easy on kids granted, but in the short term, some are just happy for the doubling up of presents and weekend visits to contraband food outlets. So, it's not all bad. Better than having two unhappy parents, fighting and making you spy on the other one's every move. Yes, divorced parents have their issues but so do married ones.

If you say no, then they say phew! But what if like me you wanted kids? Again, an insensitive response and how is it any of their business? I wanted children which was one of the reasons I got married. I saw myself having three children by the time I was 35 and working from home, home schooling them and preparing them for world domination. Forget Tiger Mum, I had a Lion Mama plan to thwart all others. Alas, he's now living that plan with Little Mrs New Boobs outside the M25. So, who is really winning here, huh?

On the question of whether someone else was involved – everyone loves to think that one of you had an affair on the other. Chances are that this didn't happen because most married people are too busy fighting to be having affairs all the time especially if they have kids. But then I do know it happens. I just don't like the interrogator's attempt at extracting gossip. If you as a woman admit to having an affair, then you are tarnished as a scarlet woman. If he had the affair, then you are the poor sap who was cuckolded by a man; or they conclude you aren't good enough in bed to keep a man. It's all very black and white in the eyes of those who judge. I note that these questions only seem to come from those who have never been married. I suppose the equivalent may be a woman who'd never given birth asking a woman with a child if giving birth hurt or not.

Question 3. The unnecessary prediction: Dating again is going to be hard. Better the devil you know. There aren't enough men out there.

Yes, the comforting words of friends and family alike. It's never easy after the death of a person, relationship or TV series (bring back *Living Single, Different World* and *Thirtysomething* please) but to be told that you are now going to struggle is the single woman's jinx. Stop saying this. *Please*!

I don't assume that dating is going to be easy. In fact, I assume it's going to be very hard because I'm older, I know what I can and cannot live with and I'm generally not enamoured by mediocrity. In addition, some of the good guys are happily married to other people and good for them. But there is no need for the doom and gloom of dating from those that aren't in the midst of it. What I will say though is that if you are in a marriage or relationship that isn't working out right now and you think being single is the solution then think twice (breaks into Celine Dion impression). Being single is a lovely thing to be when it's by choice but not when it's thrust upon you or if you're looking for another partner.

Every divorce is different and should be treated as such. I wish that I could explain what went wrong to every person that asked but I found myself, over time, reducing a seven-year relationship into headliners. I was W, he wasn't X, I wasn't Y, he was Z. That didn't do either of us justice. Anyway, he's remarried now so clearly being married to me didn't put him off the institution for very long. So, let's not judge the divorced unless like so many I've met they aren't divorced or been anywhere near a divorce lawyer. Ask them to tell you the difference between a *decree nisi* and *absolute* and if they don't know, assume they're lying. In which case, judge away!

2. The Home

efore I could even contemplate dating, I had to move out of the ex-marital home. There are a few things I need to share first. I hate packing. It's one of those activities that fill me with dread. Therefore, I don't enjoy going on holiday and I don't enjoy moving to a new house. It takes me forever to settle into a new location and I'm not one for feeling unsettled. I'm a homebody, a typical Taurean and fundamentally quite lazy. I am also a hoarder. Not just clothes but books, DVDs, VHS tapes that I one day plan to convert into DVDs, CDs, more books, magazines that I half read but want to cut out articles from and err, yes, even more books. So, when I split up with Starter Husband it took me a while to get out of there into my shoe box. At one point, I even tried to convince Starter Husband that instead of me moving we could split the house into two flats and live happily ever after with the kids running in between the two. Those were the days when Starter Husband had tricked me into thinking I could still have his sperm post-divorce. He changed his mind though not long after I moved out. But I digress... back to the story. Ah yes, The Move.

The Move

This isn't as easy as it sounds. When people talk about divorce, they don't tell you that there will be financial winners and losers. I was the loser in most ways. His life carried on exactly as it had before. Same job, same house, same routine. He just didn't have to buy as much chocolate or keep the heating up to 25 degrees. I insisted on my chocolate slightly melted and walking around semi-naked at all times of the day. I know! Most men would have loved this. So, for him the divorce wasn't as unsettling as it was for me. My mum tried to convince me to keep the house and not buy the flat, but I wasn't keen on living in the house alone with a car I couldn't drive. No if I was going to be single again then I wanted to do it fabulously and that just wasn't Ealing.

The search for the next home started and I realised that suburbia wasn't for me. It was great when I was looking at school league tables and planning escape trips to towns on the M3 and M4 but as a Singletini, these were less attractive. A lazy Sunday lunch in Winchester is lovely when you're married but I would die of boredom doing it alone. Nobody to people watch with. I started looking at property websites and somehow decided that Knightsbridge was an option. I wanted to live near Harvey Nicks and be Eddy from *Absolutely Fabulous*. My Patsy would have to come later as bestie was already married. Somehow the places were in budget if I didn't mind paying cash and moving into a cupboard with a 10-year lease. I remember going house hunting with ex-hubby who seemed unusually helpful in driving me around to potential homes and me bursting into tears because I couldn't afford anything. I think my tears bought me an extra nine months at our old place if I'm honest. Bless men, they hate tears. But these were genuine. I was too old to start again despite Mama Black seeing this as an opportunity to get a new housemate. Two single girls out on the town, *Thelma and Louise* style. I didn't have the heart to break it to her that the film didn't end well. Besides, she has her own Thelma.

28

And so, I explored London. I went to meet dodgy men in High Street bought suits who called themselves estate agents in areas as far flung as Plumstead, Peckham and (I find this hard to admit) Thornton Heath. But none of them made my heart sing. I pranced around my ex's house semi-naked, occasionally refreshing the property websites but mainly lamenting my situation. I realised that South London wasn't going to work for me. There were not enough tube links and as a conscientious non-driver (I chose drinking over driving at university and rarely regret this decision) I needed to be nearer to town. East was an option but the thought of being that far away from Heathrow filled me with dread. Not only did I hate packing, but I also hated long trips to the airport. I know I could have rented somewhere in the meantime, but I didn't see why I needed to spend money on rent when I had a room in a house for free. So, what was I to do except watch my property programmes religiously and hope that the one bargain that Kirstie and Phil found on *Location, Location, Location* that no one else wanted would come up soon?

And then I saw it. My shoebox. I can't explain why I fell in love with the shoe box. It was a basement flat and I'm a child of the sun. The Feng Shui master that came to visit kept tutting at it and saying it would never work for me. It was nowhere near the tube stations (yeah that dodgy Overground to nowhere useful doesn't count) and it was full of damp. But I could walk to Harvey Nicks! Yes, it would take me over an hour as I tend to get distracted along the way, but it was doable – and it would be mine. I could get black cabs Carrie Bradshaw style from outside my house. Well, I'm a black girl often dressed in fancy dress and dangerously high heels so only every third cab stops but… it's the dream. People would be impressed by the address until they saw it but I didn't care. Oh, and it had a garden. Today, I share part of it with the grumpy neighbour upstairs and in the 12 years I've been here I've never used it but at the time it was a great selling point. I should use the garden more...

It wasn't easy my singirls. Firstly, it was more than I could afford and as a workshy person I had spent the last year doing very little whilst recovering from a marriage breakdown. So, I did what anyone would do in my situation. I guilt tripped my ex-husband, mother and sister into lending me the extra money. Luckily, their desire to stop listening to me moan about moving was enough for the bank transfers to happen pretty quickly.

So, ex-hubby who was suspiciously supportive of me moving to Peckham packed up all of my belongings into the back of Ronnie the Mini Cooper and four trips later I was moved in. He wrote me a lovely card telling me that if ever I needed anything done, I could call on him subject to gaining permission from Little Miss New Boobs; he then quickly disappeared from my life.

The key was that now I could date and have sex in my space again. This had been, I thought, the one thing stopping me from dating up till that point. Goodbye suburbia, hello shoebox girl. The move was finally done. It took me years to unpack mind you but finally I had moved on.

The Plumber's Nightmare

I'm a rogue plumber's dream, i.e., the customer who doesn't have a clue about what to ask or how something is meant to work and doesn't really care. I just want it fixed. To this day I still don't know how the heating system works and I am constantly surprised in equal measure when it works and when it breaks down. I'm not proud of this but this is one of the few jobs my exes had all done well so I let them do it whilst I sat on the sofa, eating snacks and watching reality TV. Don't judge, my singirls. My slagging off TV wannabes was contributing to the relationship in its own way and my exes were happy that I wasn't bossing them for once.

So, the thing is that I'd *just* moved into my first flat that I'd bought all by myself (sort of) and the whole thing, whilst exciting, was also pretty daunting. Then like all new buys, things started to go wrong. The wiring was like something out of a bad horror movie and I'm easily spooked. The smell of damp that had been masked by the estate agents enveloped me the moment I walked in and the boiler that had been working perfectly fine was now constantly on the blink. Why was this happening to me? I remember thinking this was relationship karma giving my balls a squeeze until my Dad told me that buying a property is like having a baby. After the initial exhilaration, the first two years are full of worry, sleepless nights and leave you broke.

Firstly, it was a Victorian conversion. I know I should have thought about this, but the Victorians lived an awfully long time ago and whilst the properties are really pretty and quite robust…they are old. Apparently, the boiler was also from that era or thereabouts and was a nightmare to fix. I can't stand the cold, and must have a hot shower in the mornings and a hot two-hour bath at night. In summer, a lack of hot water meant I was no good for the people on the tube, at work, the nation or the entire universe for that matter.

I had three plumbers come 'round costing me no less than £300 each and who tutted, banged around a lot then told me that I was going to have to get a new boiler costing thousands of pounds. I had just purchased a flat I could ill-afford. Where did they think I was going to find the money? That's when I learned that certain postcodes are not such a blessing. Inflated prices were the plumbers' way.

Secondly, there was a leak between my flat and the one upstairs. After much investigation it turned out that it was neither their nor my fault but that of the evil freeholder. He was the most elusive man in England – probably because he makes his money by ignoring his tenants and leaseholders and swanning off on safaris to Kenya which is where I finally tracked him down. As I stared at the ugly hole that was now in my ceiling, I felt myself fall into a first-time buyer's pit of despair. I was in between contracts and was never going to find the money to deal with these massive jobs.

And then strangely enough it was the power of Facebook that saved me. My status updates about my plumbing woes caught the attention of the guy from the *Foodie Call* blog who said that he had a friend who was a gas engineer. I spoke to him and, lo and behold, he didn't patronise me. Not once. He told me to call British Gas and get them to come out. I thought this was going to be more expensive and how could they fix it if it was already broken? No, they could, they would just charge for it. So, I did as I was told (for once) and that's when Stu came into my life.

He was in his 20s, a smoker (I forgave him) who looked at my Pottinger's boiler and declared that it still had a good few years left in her yet. He didn't lie. I had it for three more years. I welled up as he told me I would only have to go without hot water for one more day. Stu looked a little perplexed at this mad, black woman who wept at the thought of hot water, but he had no idea what pains I'd been through. I hate the cold with a passion and I had been forced into wearing clothes in my own home. No half-naked dancing which was probably a good thing anyway as I hadn't bought curtains yet. Hot water and heating are essential for my mental state as my exes will testify. I can't even have sex if the temperature of the room isn't at least 25 degrees. It's a blessing and a curse, my singirls. Warm muscles don't pull.

So, a big thank you to British Gas Stu who really was my angel in blue. Oh, I've had many others, but none have ever come close to comparing to you or getting me to write poetry.

The Tool

There are many useless appliances in my flat such as the hand-held blender, five different heat stylers for my hair and the iron that barely gets used. I've never owned a power drill though. I thought about buying one but when I looked in

Argos, they didn't have any in pink and the others just looked too phallic. They were too big and serious for a power tool virgin like me. I couldn't see myself drilling and enjoying it without the appropriately matching outfit so eventually I decided that this was one item I could live without.

Then I bought a desk which now sits in various pieces in the office simply because the instructions say it needs a power drill to assemble. I may be a self-professed feminist but I still have flashbacks of me struggling to put together the bed that the John Lewis delivery man said would take an hour to assemble. Half a day and a trip to the chiropractor later I was looking at a skewed bed and left-over parts. It still can't take too much weight on it which given the amount of time I spend on it, isn't a good thing. I bought that bed in good faith expecting it to arrive looking exactly as it did in the photograph! Never again, I told myself and yet here I was with yet another John Lewis trick – the desk.

Somehow, I decided that this was going to be my glass slipper. It's always hard to choose who to see when you have options. The guy that could come over with a power drill and put up this desk for me would be my DIY prince charming. After all, aren't we meant to find partners who complement us? I clearly like to shop and buy things I can't assemble. Ergo, I need an assembler.

An easy task you may think. I thought so too. I was convinced that most men would proudly own a power drill. In fact, I was surprised that there were no photos on dating sites with men in tool belts and not much else. Guys take note. This is a cheaper, more effective means of pulling than hiring that fake fireman's costume or photoshopping in some abs. Trust me fellas, this would get you *soo* many dates.

It turns out that finding a man with a good power drill is harder than finding an online date under six feet tall that doesn't lie about his height. This didn't make sense to me. I remember many a dull trip to B&Q with the ex to find that one screw that would raise his shelving to such heights that we invited the family over for viewings. I also remember the many times I collapsed from sheer boredom on these trips. I don't mean they have to be DIY obsessive as that is as dull as gym-obsessed men. I mean, I have pots and pans that have never seen boiling water. So surely someone has drills and DIY stuff that they hardly use? Mind you, my pots are pretty.

There was the one guy who said that he could do it for me. I was impressed. Then he revealed that I would have to wait until he was back at work as he didn't actually own the tools and he'd never done anything like this before. Two power tool virgins attempting to assemble a desk. I envisaged myself tweeting away at my desk before it promptly collapsed, so I politely declined. My home insurance doesn't cover naiveté.

Then there was the youngster who boasted about his drill and said that not only would he lend it to me but that he could even assemble the desk for me. I had never even imagined assembling it myself but I smiled sweetly and we made plans for two days hence. Sadly, on that fateful night he lost the ability to use his fingers or phone as I haven't heard from him ever again. I'm guessing that would preclude him from using a drill. What a tool.

Eventually I left the desk to one side but I did manage to hang a mirror and a picture with the help of a girlfriend. And I ordered a pink power drill online which never arrived. Finding this elusive man clearly wasn't happening. I seriously hoped that this wasn't a sign of things to come. Or maybe I read the signs wrong. I guess a girl must be open to the fact that sometimes her prince charming may come in the right packaging but need assembling.

3. The Body

*L*ike some women I spend way too much time worrying about what other people think about my body. I don't know why, as most people are too busy worrying about their own looks to care about mine. Maybe being single again focuses your attention on how marketable you are. I had sort of sorted out the dating space as in the flat where I could drag them back to but not what I was selling, as in me. I would love to tell you that I joined the gym and lost eight kilos in three months but alas my body denial is far, far deeper than that. It took 12 months to get it into decent shape after all that relationship disrepair. Don't be scared. It wasn't that bad. It just means that I wasn't boring everyone with diet woes online and turned to a predominantly alcohol-based diet for a while.

My Pretty Woman Moment

One day whilst out shopping I had a 'Julia-Vivienne-Roberts-moment'. There are scenes from the film *Pretty Woman* that are imprinted on my mind: the bit where Vivienne is in the red dress at the opera, the bit where he (Robert Gere) climbs the fire escape, that hotel piano scene and the one where she's walking towards his car and Kit says, "Work it baby, work it, work it. Own it!" I also love the bit where she says, "I say who, I say when I say... *who!*" Yes, it's safe to say that I'm a fan of the film. Sue me! I grew up in the '90s.

My 'moment' alas was of the 'snobby-shop-keeper-on-Rodeo-Drive' variety. As was often the case, on my way home I got distracted by the shops on the King's Road. On this day, I spotted this gorgeous dress in a window, so I went in and asked if I could try it on.

"You do realise that it's a size eight?" the shop assistant exclaimed, looking me over with disbelief.

I nodded eagerly and explained that yes, if I get flu and don't eat for 14 days straight, I too am a size eight... on top. Clearly, she wasn't fooled once she caught a glimpse of my African heritage... but the dress puffed out from the waist. Honest!!

"And I think I should tell you that it's quite expensive?"

Well, my singirls, that was it. This woman had looked at my dazed and confused fashion sense and judged me as not being able to afford said dress. Carefully considering which of my cards I could put it on and whether or not I remembered any of my pin numbers, I figured I might as well do the 14-day fast now. Of course, there was no Richard Gere in sight with a platinum credit card when you need one. It was just me and the nervous guy in the CD collection section with the greasy hair and smelly dog. Oh, did I mention that this was a charity shop? Maybe Richard Gere types don't do charity shops.

I was feeling confident and resolved that I wasn't going to be defeated by a piece of fabric. All was going swimmingly until... I had to zip it up. I popped my head out of the changing room and humbly asked for someone to help me. Thankfully, the smelly dog guy had gone.

I won't describe the tussle that ensued, my singirls, because it's just too embarrassing. I will say that it took all three shop assistants including Basement Bob from the basement to do the zipper up. I feigned calm, fought back tears and attempted not to breathe in, cursing the panini I'd munched for lunch and claiming (not for the first time) that I had IBS (irritable bowel syndrome).

Realising that the dress nearly fit and that they were close to a sale, the shop assistants changed their attitude pretty quickly. I now had the age-old dilemma: buy the dress I couldn't quite fit into or afford or just tell them where to stuff their gorgeous dress and their boutique attitudes?

Let's just say I am now the proud owner of a fuchsia David Fielden silk dry clean only dress which needs a team to get on. Erm... who's David Fielden? I asked myself the same question. But I won my singirls, I won! And that's what counts when you're having a 'Pretty Woman moment'. The happy ending.

… Or maybe Vivienne (Julia Roberts) was talking to me when she said, "Big mistake, big, huge!"

The Fashion Hoarding Optimist

Every time I read a magazine in springtime, the advice is to clear out my wardrobe and throw out anything I haven't worn in six months. Six months! I have new clothes that I haven't worn in three years. Damn, I still have my first Levi's jacket from when I was 15. I still have my first bra! Yes, my singirls, my name is Chelsea and I'm a fashion hoarding optimist. I know this because:

1. I believe that I can slim into anything. Yes, I haven't been a size six in over 10 years, but they are always on the sale racks. It's rude not to take them home. I should remember that 6 is my shoe size not my dress size.

2. I conveniently forget I'm African and have the butt to prove it. You know how Charlize Theron's dress slinks onto the floor in that advert? Or in every film where a woman is trying to seduce a man? Well I do it, it slinks…then sits stubbornly on my hips. My secret fear is that if I was with a group who got stuck on a desert island I may be sacrificed first, and they would live off my butt for a few months.

3. I believe I can make anything into something fabulous. Like the men I date, all clothes have potential. However, superglue is my friend as I failed Domestic Sciences. I don't know how to knit, sew or crochet. I blame this mainly on being left-handed and my mother claiming it was harder to teach me.

4. Sales and second-hand are my retail temptations. I can't resist a bargain or something that has a history.

5. I believe that all fashion trends will eventually come back into style if I just hold out, so I keep everything. At school, my mum bought me blue Doc Marten-like shoes two years before they trended. This gave me a false sense of my ability to spot a trend.

6. I believe that anything I like will never go out of fashion. Fuchsia is the new black. I've been fuchsia-basing for 12 years now.

7. My bathroom cabinet mirror lies to me *all* the time. Facebook photos on the other hand, don't. I think it's time I got a full-length mirror

8. I believe that I may gain weight at any moment, so I keep three wardrobes at all times. One for the real me, one for the size six me that will never be and one for the fat me I fear I may one day be.

But one summer I decided that I was going to accept their challenge and wear my clothes or throw out anything that I hadn't worn in over six months… OK a year… OK two years. Baby steps. I couldn't justify three different wardrobes. No wonder I had no space for anyone else to move in.

And, I did try my singirls. Dinner at Shanghai Blues in Holborn and I wore my vintage stiletto Prada heels, figure hugging PVC-like pants and a halter neck top. I did a cursory jiggle in the mirror and left my flat *sans* the flat shoes. I know, my singirls, but I wanted to use my tiny denim Guess handbag and they wouldn't fit.

I took a taxi to the tube station but when I got there the stilettos kept getting caught in the escalator staircase gaps. I felt decidedly wobbly and cursed not taking that 'walk-in-high-heels' course more seriously. Instead the short walk to the restaurant left me shaking. I claimed hunger but I and the heels knew the real deal. I was a fake.

As I sat there discussing *dim sum*, my friend Olga alerted me to my peep show and *den sum*! An escaped nipple for appetisers wasn't on the menu. A gorgeous dinner done, and we walked to Tamarai. A gasp from Jamel and Heidi revealed that my skin-tight pants were now low riders giving me African builder's crack. I spent most of the night with my butt against the cold bar. The music was great, but I wasn't feeling secure enough in the heels to do more than a cursory jiggle. Besides, who knew what body part would escape next?

Bless, I did get one guy chat me up. He was a short Asian, Thai fighter with great abs (he made me feel them) and erm, his name was Abs. He told me I was the best-looking girl in Tamarai which was code for the girl with the most on display and most likely to go home with him. So, it's not all bad being a fashion hoard and optimistic if you like short men with blonde streaked hair and pictures of his car that he'd sold last week. I couldn't risk it. There was no way I was going to be able to get home on public transport.

Three words of advice though: bra, belt and blister cream. Some clothes had never been worn for a reason. The next day I threw the top on the 'for charity shop' pile and bought a belt. But I wonder if I should just superglue furry trimming onto those heels and try again? I'm guessing that's not what the designers at Prada intended.

Rest assured that no shoes were hurt or damaged when writing this. Just my dignity. I clearly hadn't learned the art of sexy dating chic so added it to my list of things to do pre-dating. The list was getting ridiculously long. Not that I wasn't getting any attention. I was. I just don't think it was the sort that was going to lead to the kind of dates I wanted, and I soon started to get nervous about re-entering the world of dating – and the men weren't trying to make it any easier.

The Butt Effect

The problem with being blessed with curves, my singirls, is that some men think it's OK to make an unsolicited approach in public. I say this as my recent chocolate-induced weight gain has all been suitably placed on my most African part. Not ideal admittedly but a curse that I have accepted as mine – that some men will beep their horns or approach me only from behind. However, it has become dull.

Gone are the days when they even pretend to be interested in my personality. I do still have one. I'm more than just one part of my anatomy. Three incidents highlight the relationship between black men and the butt. I can't comment on other races as I've never been exposed to their views.

My work colleagues

I was on the Victoria train on the way down to Brighton for a meeting when a guy stumbled into our carriage, cut me off in mid-flow when I was intricately explaining why I deserved a raise to my boss and his PA, and told me that his friend wanted to talk to me. I said that I was busy as my white colleagues looked on baffled. But no. He had the persistence of a dog with a new bone and insisted that I talk to them before they got off the train at East Croydon. Now I recall them walking behind us on the train platform. Coincidence? I think not. The PA gently asked me later if this was a common thing. I told her that it was a black-man-and-butt thing and that they really didn't discriminate. I could see from her reaction that she would have liked this to happen to her – kind of like the same way I wanted that raise. We can't always get what we want though.

The grabber

Saturday on Oxford Street is an assault course at the best of times as we know, but this time I felt a definite grab of the butt. Turning around, a tall black guy smiled at me and acknowledged that yes, that was him. He seemed rather proud of himself whilst pretending to be shy. Though resigned to that behaviour, I was annoyed; my friend Linda was not impressed and started having a go at him. His retort, delivered with a smile was, "I saw something I liked." Apparently, there is no shame or grabbers remorse in this world. It made me realise how complacent I'd become about this sort of behaviour. A wedding band had saved me from it for so long that I'd forgotten. And yet if he'd grabbed someone's breasts it would have played out completely differently. The sexual touching laws need work.

Shh... I'm praying

Some people have church, the bath or bookshops as their special place. I have HMV. A place I go to worship the musicians and directors who will give me hours of joy. So needless to say, I wasn't too impressed when a young man saw me walk by and started making 'whoop whoop' noises at his friend. His approach was immature at best and I knew he was completely inappropriate when he bragged that he was 28. Again, he expected me to congratulate him over what was basically the end of male puberty.

Purely out of pity, my singirls, and a keen understanding of the fact that you never know when there will be a man recession, I took his number. These are the times when we need to put aside our prejudices and be appreciative that young men exist. Just not in HMV! I never called him mind you as he'd broken the cardinal rule of approach which is demonstrating an uncontrollable need to entertain his sniggering friends.

The strange thing is that men love to tell me that I will miss this behaviour when I'm old and my butt has gone south, and no one takes a glance at that continent. But I doubt it. Being objectified is exhausting. I'm constantly second-guessing their motives and taking compliments as insults when they make their overtures. Oh well, my singirls, back to those glute-building leg lifts for me.

The Chocolate Breakup

During the divorce, I had another much more emotional breakup – the one with chocolate. We were at my graduation ceremony. This was supposed to be a joyous day and I was feeling somewhat happy and a little snug in my suit. My parents were there and as I pulled my skirt down again Mama Black asked me what I had been eating lately. I looked at her and admitted that my chocolate intake had gone up a tad since the breakup but that I had it under control. Her face said otherwise. As everyone else cheered on their graduates my mum told me that I had indeed gained weight. Perfect timing Mama Black.

The diet wasn't something that I particularly wanted to do. Then my mother kindly pointed out that I needed to lose weight if I was ever going to get another man and therefore give her the grandchildren I had denied her by selfishly getting divorced. To be told that I was fat was too much at this point. I know some of you can rock the fat chic look but on my five-foot-five frame I just look pregnant. In fact, I'd already been offered a seat on the tube... *twice*. So, it was time for action. And not being one to do things by halves, I went full in.

There are breakups and then there are food breakups. The first I have learned to manage with aplomb. A few sad songs, lots of analysis with friends and writing evil tales of revenge mean that I get over most breakups in a matter of days. OK, sometimes it takes weeks but there are only so many times I can play certain tracks before the neighbours threaten to feed me to the foxes. But chocolate? It wasn't going to be easy.

And so, I embarked on a year of no chocolate. This was after being on two to three a day for the previous three years. Let's just call it relationship weight. I toppled the scales at a figure so unsexy that I realised that this may have been part of the reason I was struggling to get a date. I looked awful and wasn't feeling particularly sexy. I started jogging, cut out the chocolate and took in warm salads every day to work. And the results were instant. I dropped 21lbs and was so close to that elusive size eight that I decided to celebrate... with chocolate.

I don't regret my year without it as it allowed me a chance to reflect on when I craved it most; it tended to be when I was bored or when I was celebrating something or when I was trying to console myself or... well, basically whenever I thought about it. I was like a pubescent boy with sex.

Inevitably we had a long reunion when the year was up. I dove straight in there and like old lovers who knew each other's bodies, we embraced and have barely let go since. But I'd tasted sexy. I tasted size eight and I knew that I was somewhat ready to go out there and taste a mate. To chocolate!

The Chocolate Penny Drops

Here was what had dawned on me slowly but surely...the last time I'd dated was years before, and I had been a lot younger, a lot more open to the foibles of men and a lot less worried about having children someday. All the time I'd been looking at things like moving into the flat and my size holding me back from dating but I really wasn't doing anything about it. Instead I was burying myself in post-divorce denial. This denial suggested that I wouldn't be single for long because men were able to see through the badly-fitting clothes and two extra stone but apparently, despite being the visual creatures they are, this wasn't happening (I was going through an extreme tomboy phase which consisted of three pairs of trousers and football shirts. Admittedly now I realise that it wasn't a good look, but I was always comfy).

I don't know what I expected from dating but I had never had to work at it before. I would just prance around a club and *hey presto* a man would appear who would ask me out on a date. But time had been cruel to me. There was now the internet and with it, men had plenty of options. They didn't have to work so hard and they also had access to porn whenever they wanted. There was no sense of urgency or desire anymore. Suddenly things had switched and hey, men had the dating power which is intrinsically linked to access to sex.

I did once meet a guy at a club who wanted to date me. Of course, after having lived with someone for ages, I knew the things I could tolerate and those that would lead to me searching for methods of murder online. This guy sniffed of undetectable poison options. He was nice but I soon realised that he had a temper and that he was likely to start an argument at the drop of a hat. Once, he'd started an argument with an estate agent who was driving us round looking for a new flat for my sister. He did this because he knew what we wanted better than we did after only having just met us. That's how he treated me in the relationship – like he knew better and was just waiting for me to accept it. Nah!

And so, it dawned on me that my dating confidence had taken somewhat of a knock and it was not what it used to be. I knew how to date pre-app but this was where the rules had changed, and I was no longer a student who had no designs on their sperm.

I decided that I needed a strategy. That's right, I needed a plan because this wouldn't do. A life on my own was not a life for me. I was born to have little people to boss around. Why didn't anyone see this but me? As my friend Linda kindly told me, she didn't think I was particularly maternal. I had a load of godchildren so not sure why not, but I believed myself to be a future mum.

But first I would wallow in chocolate and self-pity for a while longer. As I said, I'm a slow learner and there was something about internet dating and dieting that didn't feel right. I think it was the fact that both required effort and I was suffering from post-relationship fatigue. When the chocolate penny dropped, I picked it up and ate it because I believe in the three-second rule. I bounced around for a few more months until ... the universe decided to throw me a taste of what could be.

46

4. Getting Back Out There

I started talking to men again I guess but it was all a bit tentative and if the truth be told whilst I was bigger, I wasn't really interested in them at all. But these were the men who in their own way gave me the dating confidence I would need in the soon-to-come dating world. I don't think any of them knew it at the time, but they played a pivotal role in helping me decide how and who I would date. So, a big thank you to them.

The beauty of dating again is that you can see your likes and dislikes more clearly. I think you become less tolerant as you become older which is inversely proportional to your desire to be in a relationship. The thing is that after a long relationship you only have that as a marker for what you want and don't want in a relationship, so early dating experiences are about figuring out what it is you will tolerate and what will have to be put down as being fussy. Here are some of mine.

Going, Going, Gone

One night I was out in Westbourne Park at a club listening to… house music. This was not my idea clearly and I was there on a mission to entertain some overseas visitors with a friend. And then, I saw him. A cute guy with a unique mix that I can't mention in case I identified him. He was heading out of the country in the next few months and I thought yes, a quick 'Stella' fling and then he'll disappear. Who could ask for more than that? Not me. This was what my friends were telling me I needed. I could ignore the fact that he loved house music. We all have flaws.

It started off badly as this guy had the same name as the ex. I'd started to realise that there were some names that weren't for me. All the saints and apostles, most common Nigerian names and of course any Ghanaian name beginning with a K. But apart from that I'm good.

I interject to point out that I haven't really bought music since the early '90s. I feel about house the same way I do about long division. Clearly, I was off sick and missed the lesson on house music appreciation. I've made peace with this.

But then we started talking and as per usual I fell for him. My singirls, I did. He was a lovely person; he would send flowers to his mum to cheer her up and he also lived not too far from me. This was it. The one to get me back on the dating horse. I'd already imagined all three of our kids (his job commitments meant we never did get 'round to having the fourth) and was trying to imagine which sort of flowers he would buy me to cheer me up… I hoped it would be something bold and bright and easy to manage.

The problem was he was about to leave the country for a long time to shoot something amazing, somewhere exotic. My window was already limited but he always seemed so busy. He invited me for the odd drink with the gang who all grew up in the same area and were a little too incestuously close for my

48

liking, but I smiled and thought about when we were going to get some snog-a-thon time in. But then the date was pushed back and I was given another two months in which to seduce my prey.

I have to be clear here. I didn't really think it had long-term potential. Apart from the fact that I had doubts about whether he could carry me as he was a skinny thing, I was getting a little tired of the merry band of mates he hung around with. In particular, I wasn't too keen on the gym fanatic friend who used a vague connection to get closer and thought it OK to call and talk to me about his diet and exercise regime. Was this a test of my allegiance to the group? I wasn't sure and so I endured these conversations in the vain hope that it would win me some much-needed brownie points. Future Hubby also had a bit of a coke habit which I put down to his industry. I'm not a fan of toilet socials.

Then came the night I was off clubbing. I had a vague plan to meet some acquaintances at Egg in King's Cross but then *he* called. I told him of my plans, he said that it wasn't a good club but that I should come to the local pub and hang out with the gang. I wasn't that keen on another night of the girls ignoring me but figured why not. I had a great outfit on. There was no point in wasting it on a random.

And so, off I went to the pub and was totally overdressed /underdressed for the beer garden gathering that greeted me. I stood around trying to keep warm before they suggested we all go back to one of their homes in Chiswick. Finally! A radiator I could hug was in my future as well as some couch time with him.

My excitement quickly dissipated when I realised that the cosier location was so that they could have yet another coke party. Was I seriously the only person who didn't do coke? Alas no, his gym friend also abstained. I'm guessing there was a chance that it would clash with his steroids. And so, the two abstainers sat there as the rest of them had a coke party. I know I should have made my excuses and left but I was still hopeful.

Finally, the night started to wind down and it was agreed that three of us would get a taxi home – me, my Stella and Gym who I was really starting to hate. It made sense for us to drop him off first but then I realised that I'd made a tactical error. By talking to Gym for so long I'd given my Stella the impression that I may have been into him. And so, as the taxi pulled up and someone discovered another wrap of coke, he ran up the cab and said he was staying behind, leaving me in a cab with Gym talking about protein shakes.

I was devastated for a few days because I'd invested way too much imagination and brain time on this one. But then it hit me. Any guy who was willing to choose a line of coke over sex with me clearly wasn't someone who would be able to keep me satisfied for long anyway. And so, it was with little regret that my first potential post-marriage fling didn't happen.

It was beginning to dawn on me that this dating thing was going to be harder than I thought but I knew I didn't want to get drawn into a 'trustafarian' group of coke meetups. It just wasn't me. Next!

The Waiter

As my birthday was looming, I realised that my life plan had gone remarkably wrong. I was in the middle of an amicable divorce, wasn't making any money (the creative entrepreneurial journey) and was heavier than anyone my height should be without booking two seats on the train. One for me and one for the snacks. OK, I was never that big, but I felt like I was. When you're not tall even a little extra weight sits on you differently I guess.

So, what's a girl with no money or honey to do? Simple. I was going to blow the last few hundred that I had on a holiday using the credit card my soon-to-be-ex didn't know I still owned. Yup, I was taking this emotional train wreck on a road trip. Maybe it was watching too many episodes of *Property Abroad* programmes that did it, but I was inspired.

The thing is I really hate travelling at the best of times so after my initial excitement, I soon decided that staying at home would be the better option. I could finally get to watch all the programmes I'd been taping religiously whilst I slept in until *Loose Women* started at noon every day. I found myself worrying about the strangest of things like, 'I never did finish watching *Homes Under the Hammer*. Did they get the old B&B with slight damp in Bournemouth?' Nope, I told myself, I figured I had way too much to do at home.

But my soon-to-be-ex, spotting an opportunity to have the house to himself for a few days, wasn't having it. He searched for destinations which involved me getting on planes and even bought me a Jasper Conran suitcase. It was black and pink. I couldn't resist the thought of taking it out for a spin. He stopped short of helping me pack mind you.

This was during my lame attempt at learning Portuguese. It lasted longer than my gym memberships but shorter than the average hairstyle. I finally decided on the island of Porto Santo. Cape Verde was too expensive and too far for this chick and I'd heard that Madeira was full of old people. Porto Santo, an island next to the island of Madeira, sounded perfect.

So, I arrived, promptly climbed into bed and switched on the TV. The island was lovely but I wasn't really one for sight-seeing and it was colder than I'd packed for despite it being April. Laptop in bag, I decided this was the holiday I was going to start writing. So many ideas, so little motivation but it was time to pull out that literary masterpiece that every English Lit major feels lives in them. Fuck it – there was a minibar. I'd start tomorrow.

That night I went down to dinner and as I sat contemplating bland hotel food, I noticed a waiter noticing me. I dismissed it. A single woman going on holiday and getting it on with a barman or waiter was so last decade. He came over and introduced himself. He was from Mozambique and his accent was just too cute. Lifting trays all day had also been very kind to his biceps. I fought the temptation that was fuelled by a weakness for men that look like they could lift me effortlessly. However, I was *not* going to be the cliché soon-to-be-divorced-woman who picks up a holiday lover.

Turns out that I was. He was lovely. He invited me out after dinner and said he would show me the island. Recognising the fact that I may have to leave my room if only to replenish the minibar, I finally accepted his invitation. I don't think I saw more than two bars and some rickety steps on the beach where The Waiter and I got better acquainted. I still think sex on the beach is overrated but sex on the rickety steps on the beach was truly delicious and sand (if not splinter) free.

For four whole days that man spoiled me. I didn't pay for a thing and he treated me like a queen. But having watched my fair share of daytime TV, I was waiting for the downside. Would he wait until I got back to the UK before begging me for money? Would he steal my passport on the last day leaving me stranded on an island without a Nando's? I had visions of me on *Richard and Judy* explaining why I had accepted a pink purse as a gift which had been secretly stuffed with cocaine. I wasn't going down like that my singirls, oh no. Prison jumpsuits would make my butt look enormous. I wouldn't survive the fashion shame.

But no. Instead he woke me up with breakfast in bed every morning, took me out to locals-only restaurants and kept me up all night with the best sex I'd had in years. I truly needed this.

Alas, I knew the rules of holiday dalliances. He was happy on the island and I was going back to the realities of London life. It was just what the divorce doctor ordered though – besides, I never did quite get the hang of Portuguese.

The Waiter certainly restored my faith in romance and men. I came back to the UK determined to throw myself into the dating game with the same openness and honesty he'd shown me. The only cliché I had to avoid was being the bitter divorced woman who didn't trust men. Besides, it was time to move on. My ex wanted the house back. My dating adventure had truly begun.

Update: As I write this, I just checked on Facebook and those arms are still looking good. Hmm… they say a ship that sails backwards never sees the sunset but maybe, just this once I'll make an exception? Darn it, he's in a relationship. Never mind.

5. The Internet

I'm one of those people who's always behind with technology. Whether it be mobile phones, laptops or any other techy stuff, I trail behind everyone else hoping that someone, somewhere will make a foolproof gadget that will be so user friendly that all I have to do is press one button and it works. I'm just not that interested in how things work and the latest techno toy. So, the potential for dating on the internet had never really crossed my mind.

But alas, times had changed and with it my dating habits had to change too. I would love to say that I threw myself into it with heart and soul but sadly this wasn't the case.

The Butt Kick

Yes, there was a time my singirls, when I couldn't get a date for love or money. Separation agreed I still needed to 'get back out there' as everyone put it and start the bloody dance of the terrible one-liners.

But back out where? The dating scene had changed beyond my recognition. I, like most of those who married in their 20s, hadn't dated properly since my university days. Back then, when I was bored with the current pickings on campus, I would simply pick another module on another campus. Please note a major in African Feminist Literature is perhaps not the best degree to finding good dating stock. I should have done what some of the women did and thought ahead. Engineering and Medicine was scattered with women who were there to meet their FuHu and so never work a day in their grown-up life. So I left university with a BA degree which included modules in Zoology, Chemistry and French all of which I can't remember now or put to good use. I'm able to dissect a frog mind you.

Back in the last millennium I would just go out to bars with my single friends, but now I was surrounded by friends who were surrounded by nappies. I had to face facts; after a long relationship I was basically not dating fit. The internet had come and passed me by. I had just about learned how to text properly on my Nokia. Remember them? Yes, it was that long ago. My soon to be ex-husband however had somehow managed to keep his techy skills up, mainly through porn so was a whizz at navigating the web. I was staring at a lot of TV nights in. But you know me my singirls, I'm nothing if not determined. I was not going to let him win. I mean, I needed to 'get back out there.' But where to start?

Like a good African girl, I went to the one place I knew I would get unbiased advice: my father. Bless him he told me to wait as my prince would come. Did he not know that a young divorcée was not really the rage? He argued that I was smart, and I argued that unless he was willing to pay for a boob job, smarts weren't really selling well on the dating market. So, I was left with no other option but to go to my biased advice option. Mama Black. She half-listened to my tales of woe, tried to convince me of seducing my ex into at least giving her grandkids, then dragged me upstairs.

At first, I thought this was yet another 'put-down-the-chocolate' conversation; however, instead of turning right into the bathroom, she took me to the spare room and the computer. There began my dating journey. This woman had accounts to them all. Dating Direct, Loopy Love (where she met a guy who had a thing for women with one leg – that was a short subscription) Meetic, Match.com and much, much more. Overload. Was I supposed to join them all?

Apparently so. My mum is nothing if not focused on her goals:

1. Getting grandchildren she can spoil incessantly and set up against us at whim.
2. Reminding me that by the time she was 30 she had three kids under five. I was already losing.
3. Getting me a man whose sperm would not embarrass her in her grandma circles. The woman seemed to be able to look at a profile and know whether he was going to 'shoot cute.' Many of those with similar interests didn't make the cut.

I went away and figured that in time I would find the energy to start dating again. I wasn't ready to shop online for a date. But Mama Black wasn't having any of it. No sooner had I reached home I'd received a cut and paste of a conversation she was having with a younger guy, aged 42.

"Bit young, isn't he?" I asked her.

"NOT FOR ME, FOR YOU!" she shouted back.

Bless her, she is great on dating sites, but Caps Lock still defeat her. I read through the conversation where she was plugging me to a stranger who wasn't my type at all. I now realise she did this on purpose to kick me into action.

So, I reluctantly asked my ex to take some semi-decent photos of me. He, recognising that this may mean my butt dent was finally going to pop from his couch (as I was still popping over for nights in and to get fed), seized the chance and took great photos. I mean so great that my dodgy write up was ignored and guys just commented on the pictures.

And thus began my online dating tales. Now I regret to admit that I'm a pro. I can write profiles for friends, spot a dud at line four and know that two inches should be taken off anything with measurements – three if it's below the waistline.

Hmm, I wonder if I have a future career as an online dating private investigator?

The Dog Whisperer

There are guys that play the online dating game with finesse. And then there are those that go for women who haven't got a clue. I think he was the latter and I was only just wising up to this whole online dating malarkey.

To be fair yes, I was fairly new to internet dating when I met him. He set himself apart by waxing lyrical about great writers I remembered from university but could never quote. I didn't stop to think that he may have googled it all because I was suitably impressed by his effortless chat … and his abs.

Oh, he was lush. I have a definite type, but I had just finished watching *Pretty Woman* and he was evoking all of my Richard Gere fantasies. He was older with peppered hair, a body that was effortlessly buff and a broody look. He ran his own successful business and sounded like a man of the world. He talked about things, not about when he was going to get into my knickers. Hmm, had I tripped on a man that was together emotionally and financially? *Yes*!

He said that he lived alone in North London and was keen to talk and make sure that we were compatible before meeting. He was clear, he wanted more than just a casual relationship and was ready to commit. This was a novel approach. I was intrigued enough to go along with it.

Then he suggested that we take our conversation off the site and chat on Skype. Now I'm not the greatest fan of Skype. The problem with a Skype date is that you must think about the state of the flat in view of the camera as well as making yourself look great and remembering not to pick at your nose/eyes/ears nervously. It's an anxiety diva's nightmare. Since then I've realised that the best place to Skype from is your bed but then you have to be careful about the body slump. So many things to consider!

But, prepare I did my singirls and I ensured that the lighting was just enough to seduce without looking like I was selling my goodies online (I would like to thank the lovely guy in Peter Jones who helped me pick out a lamp). I had to look effortlessly casual at home. This meant getting out of my daytime PJs.

When he called, I answered and there he was and...he looked better in the flesh! Wearing his loose, grey muscle man T-shirt I could see and hear him typing away furiously whilst I was talking. Hold on, why was he still typing if we were Skyping?

Him (typing): "Hi, how are you?"

Me: "Fine dear but, why are you still typing? Is your mic not working?"

Him (typing): "Shh! Err, we need to be quiet."

Me: But why?

Him (typing): "...I don't want to wake the dog."

He'd forgotten that he'd told me and the dating website that he didn't have any pets. Clearly, whether he had a dog or a wife we were not a match.com. The only slight satisfaction I got was that Skype sound when you end a call. I quickly blocked The Dog Whisperer and put on *Pretty Woman* 'cos that was the closest I was going to get to a fairy tale ending.

Dick-tators!

Clearly not everything internet is positive. Yes, it's nice to engage with a whole new group of potentials but there are risks to always being accessible.

Sunday night I'd taken a bath, lathered myself up in shea butter, donned my fluffy robe (I need a new one) and prepared myself for a night of Netflix and *Judge Judy*. Don't. I find her very soothing.

My phone pings and absentmindedly I reach for it whilst laughing at some idiot who claims his car insurance lapsed two days before the accident. Looking at my phone, I am greeted by a photo of saggy balls and a desperate, eager-to-please-looking penis in my messenger. Underneath the fuckwit had written, 'Can I ask your opinion?'

Now, I am many things, but a fan of dick pics I am not. Worse is the unsolicited dick pic. We may be friends on Facebook because we have 25 mutual friends in common but that doesn't mean I want to see your little friend or your saggy balls.

I haven't had a dick pic for so long that I'd forgotten how jarring they are. They are aggressive and never sexy looking. Why do men have this desperate need to share them with female strangers? It reminds me of the time I was flashed on a train travelling into London Bridge. The initial reaction is paralysis, embarrassment, and then self-questioning. Why me? What about my face and, as my face isn't on Facebook, my avatar suggests I want to see your piss pipe? The aggression is so blatant and yet we are meant to see this as a harmless, non-violent, hello? I hate 'Hi-WYD' messages (What You Doing, in case you didn't know what that meant) but in this day and age I'd take it over a dick pic.

I don't expect there to be much sympathy for women who talk about dating and sex online but I know that this happens to nearly all women, so it's not targeted. Even if it was, nobody has asked for this. Women are rarely turned on by a photo of a penis. It's not the same as a tittie selfie so stop pushing it on us in the vain hopes that dick pics will take off. They really won't.

Forever helpful, I then thought about ways a dick pic can be improved from hiring in a stand in one to investing in lighting and a wax. His peppercorns covering his pelvic bone and balls just weren't inviting. Guys, a 'back, sack and crack' isn't just for the metrosexuals. But again, I'm not here to help those who sexually assault women even if it's deemed a nonviolent crime because it's online. It's forcing your sex onto others because that's what you want. It's a dick-tatorship I want no part of. Please, just stop and get a new hobby of harassment.

I immediately blocked him but now every time I get a bloody message, I have to hold the screen far away in case it's someone's meat and potatoes. Why!! So, thanks to Marlon in Miami Florida for reminding me of everything that's wrong with social media, poor personal grooming and inadequate lighting.

But, if you do fancy fighting back, then you could:

- Post it on his timeline and ask why he sent it. You may face some Facebook jail time but, it's worth it.

- Send it to all the family in his friends list or if he's got his job details on there then, share the love with HR and ask them to help him as clearly, he's struggling.
- Block and move on. He craves the attention and doesn't deserve it

---

CyberSEX

So there was a time when I tried cybersex. It wasn't for long as I get bored easily and few guys are great at it. But no, cybersex some years ago was a by-product of sex dating online. You would meet someone online whose torso or certain body parts you liked the look of. I realised later that these weren't always their photos but, a girl can dream.

You would have the chat, rarely get off and move onto the next one. I didn't really get what the big deal with it was, but it does give you a chance to test out your fantasies. Answer? No matter how filthy you think your imagination can be there are thousands of guys online who are filthier. So, you're OK my precious. That thing you like to do with peaches and cream, it's really not going to shock anyone.

But then one day I met a guy from match.com. Another reason match.com and I broke up. He seemed alright and said he worked in banking. Turns out he works in the admin department for a bank. Not even a bank teller dude? You don't even get to touch the money? And then he said he lived in Catford. It was never going to work. It's outside my 45-minute dating zone. So, in my mind I decided he lived in Hampstead and was a Trader. I was starting to get the hang of this suspended reality malarkey.

It started as cybersex. He loved it. I didn't. But then he was a filthy bugger who was online every night with something new he wanted to do to me. I would 'Oooh yes Daddy' and 'Yes right there' my way through a few scenarios before he'd thank me and sign off. It was all about golden showers and all this messy stuff which made me think, not in my flat. EVER! Then he suggested we Skyped. So I did the obligatory clean-up of the room, sorted out the lighting and put on the cute tight topped pyjamas that one has tucked away for such occasions. No winter onesie for me!

There were three things that messed up the cybersex. First his voice. In my mind he was a cross between the deep-voiced one in Boyz II Men and James Earl Jones. Authoritative and commanding. So who was this pipsqueak butchering the English language at every turn? Clearly, he knew how to write it and yet when he spoke, he sounded like he was auditioning for an Urban Disney voiceover.

Then his body. Apparently, that photo he had up of his torso was quite a number of years old. My guess would be that it was before they created the concept of gyms. He'd eaten his way through quite a number of tubs of Ben and Jerry's since then and for that he blamed his sedentary job.

Oh, his place was a bloody mess! How was I supposed to imagine having sex without bringing out the marigolds and industrial strength Mr Muscle? I asked him about it, and he said that he had just had the builders in. Oh, how long ago? I asked. A year ago! I politely told him that this Skype thing wasn't going to work for me. We tried to go back to writing but every time I would imagine me breaking a heel in that messy room or his squeaky voice telling me to touch him in places I really didn't want to touch.

So, keep cybersex to cyber ex my singirls and never blur those lines. The reality is much less of a turn on.

6. The Almosts

*I*think initially I was a dating optimist and saw the potential in every cute guy I met. I was trying to be open again. I knew this because some of them weren't even that cute or mildly interesting when we met. My standards were a little twisted and The Almosts reflect those that came close to being part of my life. Looking back, I think it's clear that I was still navigating my way around the dating scene and didn't ask the right questions quickly enough. I was a sucker for a guy offering me something like a smile or food. But I've learned to look beyond that… well sometimes a nice smile and some abs are all a girl really wants, right? And to be fed. A girl has got to eat.

The Jill Scott Moment

Let me start from the beginning. I met him on Facebook. I was trying to maximise my 'internetting'. The problem with this method of dating is that people read what you write and see the photos of vibrators that you post, and they think they have you all figured out. I'm more than a photo of a pink rabbit my singirls. I read his profile and he was a gym-loving African guy who liked taking pictures with his top off. Perfect... not!

But this guy seemed genuine. He was a promoter... OK so not that genuine, but it was a slow week. We started to talk and it turned out that we had lots in common professionally and socially. He liked organising events in bars and I liked drinking. We were both going to the Jill Scott concert the following week and assuming we had similar music tastes, we arranged to meet there. The plan was between the opening act and the main course we could meet. I pictured myself as the perfect palette cleanser and decided that mint green was the way to go. To the shops I went and bought a mint green polka dot dress.

Now, confession time. I'm not a Jill Scott fan. I missed that whole neo-soul era and went straight into British rock-pop instead. Sorry my singirls, I know it's hard for you to hear. But sometimes I just buy tickets because I figure it's a good night out. I realised that he was expecting a fan, so I rushed out and bought all the albums and crammed them in over two days. As I looked longingly at my Skunk Anansie collection, I told myself it would be worth it for the icebreaker alone.

My friends and I arrived at the concert and I realised that the only way to get through a whole night of neo-soul was... drunk. By the time I went to meet my promoter guy, I was slightly squiffy but even I was surprised to discover that... he was Asian? Turns out that the photos on his profile picture were taken on a holiday where he'd gotten a really good tanning and he was born in Africa as well. He was equally surprised to discover that I wasn't a Jill Scott fan. The alcohol had made me loose-lipped. We mumbled our way through a few minutes of conversation before I suddenly remembered that I had to get in the next round.

Dejected, I went to plan B and met a guy who was decidedly tastier. I know, I tasted him. He was drinking wine which I told him wasn't a good look for a red-blooded man. I was bored and trying to avoid having to pretend to be in neo-soul lover. And this was the start of a nice long on/off relationship. So, I was glad that I got those tickets. I urge you to get out there. The only men I was meeting in my flat were plumbers and online shopping delivery men. You never know who you are going to meet out. Don't forget to thank me if you find yourself a hottie.

The Interview

So, this day had started out like every other – on the tube contemplating a life committed to my electric blanket and finding DHL Husband or Hubby Number Two.

A day of interviews loomed and grabbing fruit from the café on the way I contemplated how I, Chelsea, could be stuck in some administration job hell as opposed to working in a fabulous industry with a delicious wardrobe and a personal assistant to run errands for me. OK, I just lied to you my singirls. I had a McDonald's breakfast – double sausage and egg McMuffin meal and an extra hash brown. But it wasn't all bad as I did order water as the drink.

I sat on a panel and watched people sweat and laugh nervously in Next suits whilst I planned an ensemble for a date later that week. I was leaning towards a little black dress with a pink gash but realised that it might not forgive my winter pig-out weight. I couldn't even be bothered to focus on the interviewees as they bored me with examples of how they worked well under pressure. Maxine Saj, my buddha belly, in a tight interview dress? That my singirls was working under pressure.

Then, just as I was losing the will to live, I saw him through the glass partition right in front of me: my FuHu and father of my kids, just walking into the reception! He was hot, wearing a Hugo Boss suit, a little shorter than I'd expected but he had finally arrived! Surely the universe couldn't have been so kind as to bring him here for me. He couldn't be here in the same building as me to interview for a job in my team, could he?

I quickly rushed to the bathroom to strategise. I could ask who he was at reception, but the security guard was a little deaf and tended to shout. So, I did what any self-respecting single girl would do in this situation. I sent out a prayer to every religion and non-religion and love god out there.

"If you let this hot hunk be the next interviewee, I will not eat McDonald's breakfasts for a week. OK a month."

I then pulled down my neckline for a little extra cleavage and took off the ill-fitting cardigan to accentuate my African-ness. I walked out, he smiled, and I melted. All those weeks of chanting had finally brought him to me in the most unlikely of guises: as a potential employee to boss around at my every whim.

No, he must be for me. I had been saying my Christmas prayers to Santa early that year, so I knew that finally, this year he had answered them on time. And I wasn't going to quibble over three or four inches as long as they were more than adequately substituted for in other areas. I asked him if he was my 2pm and he said that he was indeed.

As I led him up to the interview room, I asked him how his journey in had been. He explained that he had come in from Luton. Admittedly my sashay lost a little shay as I stumbled but then he smiled, and all was well with the world again. I was going to treat this interview as a date for FuHu and I knew that in that suit he would pass with flying colours. Besides, moving him away from Luton would be my gift to him.

For about 20 minutes I lived the dream. Sadly, it turned out that I wouldn't be seeing him again. His inability to blag or provide examples of his skills ruled him out as an employee or life partner. In that moment, I realised that a good suit and a smile were not enough.

So, my singirls, off to McDonald's I went where in the spirit of New Year's resolutions I only ordered one hash brown. See, I'm learning.

A Tissue Issue

Now, as you know, I'm not one of those squeamish women who run at the sight of other people's fluids or general mess. Hello, I hate cleaning and I've had more than my fair share of nights out that ended over a porcelain bowl than I can recall. But one thing I will not put up with anymore is going on dates with sick people. It's the height of selfishness to do that when you know you are highly contagious. Please people, let's stop doing this. But not this dude. No, he decided to bring me the gift of his germs.

Germs aside, I should have known he wasn't really a goer. We met on PoF – Plenty of Fish – and before you all start telling me about your cousin's friend's sister's work colleague that met her husband on PoF, I will confess that it's one of my least favourite websites. Firstly, it's free and secondly, where else would I see such a large part of the population who proudly describe themselves as having some college or their longest relationship being under a year when they are over 35? PoF is where I met many a liar and sadly some guys are so prolific at it that they've initiated conversations with me more than once without realising that we'd spoken before.

But this guy seemed different. He had a decent job for one – or at least that's what his profile said. Turns out that he had injured his back so was off work on long-term sick but seemed to spend an inordinate amount of time on his martial arts and gym activities.

I knew it wasn't going to work when he took ages to find a car parking space and then whipped out a blue disabilities badge. He proudly told me that it was his mum's and that he hadn't paid for parking in years. I was on a date with a benefits fraudster. Then he walked me through Fulham Broadway to… Nando's. I tried not to make eye contact with the staff there as they had spotted me having dinner with another guy earlier that week. My date kept snivelling and I kindly offered him a pack of tissues. But apparently, he didn't need tissues. Instead he made me endure a meal with him coughing up phlegm over a shared platter. Now you know how much I love my Nando's my singirls, but this wasn't a happy meal. I listened as he told me why the system and life were against him. Then just as I was about to put a chip in my mouth, he spluttered all over it. My meal and this date was over soon after.

Call it psychosomatic but the next evening I started feeling ill. I stayed at home cancelling another date. I didn't hear from Blue Badge Ninja for days in which time I had developed a full case of the flu. When he finally texted two weeks later, he was surprised that I wasn't up for another date. According to him, things had gone swimmingly.

So yes, it was cold and flu season and we were all sick. But if you have a cold it's better if you rearrange because there is nothing worse than sharing germs with a potential lover. Don't worry my singirls – his germs didn't kill my love for Nando's. Just their platter for a while.

The Foodie Call

I've finally figured out what you all have known for years. Food and sex are the foundation of any good casual relationship, now more commonly known as the foodie call. Two essential needs being met at once. A delicate balance of being fed and erm… being fed! You get the picture.

So, this is how mine went down. He'd been flirting online for a while. I'd only actually met him once but you know when it's special. He likes you, showers you with loads of attention, hence, it's special. Normally I would have tried to seal the deal on the night but hey, I was drunk, the club was loud and sweaty, and I may have been slightly distracted by the Thierry Henry look-a-like at the bar. I'm new at this my singirls. Don't judge.

The Thursday before, I'd come home and scanned the fridge. Hmm. Beetroot, soya milk and chocolate body paint do not a meal make. Even though I live within a mile of six supermarkets, I just couldn't be bothered to leave my house again and then come back and cook. So, I jumped online to see if there was anything happening where there was likely to be some grub. My friend Tia suggested The Westbourne but only for a quick drink. But then *he* came along. The email asked me how I was, and we started chatting. I broke it down: I had no food and I was so hungry that I was contemplating eating at the dodgy chippy conveniently forgetting the stomach cramps from last time.

Yes, I know black women are meant to be able to throw it down in the kitchen but I guess I assumed throw down meant something else entirely? Don't judge me, cooking for one isn't much fun.

He suggested that he come around and cook. I pictured him trying to rustle up something with the body paint and beetroot. It would also mean me having to clean the flat. So, I told him no. Then he counter-offered to cook for me at his place. Now this was a plan I could work with. This would mean a meal, potential sex and no laundry in the morning? *Jackpot.*

I jumped in the shower and mentally planned an outfit that screamed, 'I could wear this to work tomorrow.' Then, just as Al Green and I were hitting the dodgy high note, my stomach rumbled, and it hit me. I didn't know where he lived! So, I jumped back online and asked. He stalled for a while then eventually told me.

Catford.

So, I called my friend Tia and we headed out somewhere less South. Tia and I had a great night out at The Westbourne and I managed to grab some food. I'm all up for a foodie call my singirls but you need to have the right ingredients, and this felt like an episode of *Ready Steady Cook*. I mean, what does one really know about a potential date and, what if he couldn't cook? What if he couldn't satisfy? What if he lived outside Zone 2?

I've Got The Power

Another joyful date was a random introduction. We met through a friend of his who I was sort of chatting to but not really because I'm not into men who wear white shoes and monitor my drinking. We chatted for a few weeks and finally the guy asked to take me out. We agreed to meet in Greenwich near Cutty Sark. I know it was out of my 45-minute dating zone, but I was working in Woolwich at the time, so I allowed it.

We met up and went for Mexican. He talked about his amazing, high-paying job as an IT project manager which made my little consulting gig pale into insignificance. I won't say there was chemistry but there was enough spice and flirtation for us to make it back to his. Don't judge my singirls, it had been a slow month.

The sex was average. He needed an awful lot of union breaks, was sweaty but didn't want to relinquish dominance and I was starting to get a bit bored. This was definitely one for the last tube home, so I was conscious of the time. Then he asked me to help him out. 'Oh goodie!' I thought. A request for something kinky?

This guy needed help with... PowerPoint. Apparently, he needed to submit a presentation to his client and didn't know how to use it. I assumed he wanted to know how to use the whizzy bits that make the letters screech onto the screen on wheels but no, he simply wanted the basics on how to set up a presentation.

I put my bra back on and gave him a 15-minute master class on how to use PowerPoint for liars. All the while I was thinking, how is this dude an IT Project Manager? To be fair, his sexual performance improved afterwards, and he was able to finish me off and drive me to Plaistow tube station all in good time. Gratitude is a wonderful thing.

I know I'm too trusting. But if someone tells me they do something for a living I believe them because, why lie? I know men spend the majority of their time thinking of ways to trick women into bed but, dude, it wasn't the job title that swayed me to go back to yours. It was those arms which should be used for more than just pointing at presentations. Sadly, that wasn't enough to convince me to meet up again.

P.S. Months later, I discovered that PowerPoint had lied about much more than just his job. He wasn't divorced and he had children. The family home was in North London not East and this was a property development he was working on. Next!

7. The Crushes

C onfession: Hi, my name is Chelsea and I have a strange inability to avoid crushing. I know I'm too old for this nonsense and yet still, a guy looks a certain way, or he says something nice to me and I fall totally in lust, imagining our lives together forever. Well until the next crush comes along. I know these crushes are just a sign of my boredom and yet I persist. It's as if I can't exist without projecting some sort of love energy onto some poor unsuspecting victim who enjoys the attention but doesn't feel the same way. No, I get a pat on the head and questioned about my hot friends instead. Oh well, I never said I was perfect!

The Cosmo Trip

Some people find it strange that I don't really read women's magazines. It's a painful memory my singirls, but I remember with clarity the day I decided to divorce them all and the cocktail one in particular (I'd already outgrown the much loved 'position of the fortnight' in *More* and felt like a proper woman when reading *Cosmo*).

Typically, it related to a dreadlocked basketball player with hazel eyes and a million-dollar smile. Well, OK he was still a student so more a take-away smile but whatever, I was hooked. I did the usual thing of dragging my bookish friends down to the basketball courts for a glimpse of this butterscotch Adonis. *Cosmo* was right and perseverance did pay off because after months of hanging around, they finally took pity and included us in their circle.

Oh, the daydreams I had about this boy! I would be in heels and a tennis skirt, him in his cute, too long shorts. Sorry my singirls, but my imagination just couldn't stretch to me in trainers.

I'm going to conveniently gloss over my own attempt at joining the women's team in which they politely told me that long nails and a general disinterest in scoring on the court were not conducive to the sport. Who were they to judge? And they didn't seem particularly interested in my injury woes either. I broke two nails!

My magazines religiously advised me to tell him about my feelings. This wasn't a course of action I warmed to but, as a disciple, I felt that the army of women who wrote these magazines knew much more than I did about love… and make up. Then the magazine gods answered my prayers. A chance conversation and some feminine wiles had him back at my flat! I said a silent prayer to the goddess of agony aunts, ran my fingers through my hair and told him how I felt. He stared at me with those hazel eyes the whole time, drinking in everything I said and moved closer. I couldn't believe that all of those years of reading about other people's problems was about to pay off!

As he came closer, I prepared myself for the inevitable kiss and half-closed my eyes. Like Aerosmith I didn't want to miss a thing. But then he reeled in horror and fell sideways, knocking over my pile of magazines in an attempt to escape. Turned out my time would have been better spent investigating my target. His type was short, gamine and entirely too delicate to ever grace a basketball court. Oh, and it turned out that an escaped hair braid dangling from my sexy top was enough to send him tripping, but not into my arms. Apparently, he wasn't the brightest spark and had always thought it was my real hair.

So, by all means, read the magazines my singirls, but throw them away and do your own research so as not to trip over them at a critical moment.

I Keep on Fallin'

He was tall, dark and African, and arrogant with a vulnerable smile. I met him at a social mixer and I put on my best flirt face. I can fake it when necessary my singirls. A shared love of sport and sex meant that we were talking on a more intimate level very quickly.

After long phone calls and online chats (I think my typing speed sky-rocketed to a record beating 20 wpm) it emerged that he was in the middle of a divorce. I ignored the bitter comments that he made about women and the ex and focused on all the things he said he wanted in his future relationship. That's right my singirls, I was in a true crush mode. Divorce be damned. I'd found myself a live one! Yes, he was an accountant but that just meant that someone would be able to explain my high cocktail budget to my bank manager.

We hung out in bars, snogged like teenagers and I was floating on cloud nine. The cloud deflated a little when he told me that he wasn't going to ever marry again. He declared that he didn't want kids till he was in his 40s. I wasn't sure that my eggs were going to be able to wait that long but like me, they were willing to try. I invited him to the Alicia Keys concert which was another shared love. I introduced him to my friends Linda and Tat. Tat told me to be careful whereas Linda and I discussed christening colour schemes.

At the venue he started bitching about the seats. His words were, "Next time I see her I want to be in the front row and looking straight up her skirt. I want to be able to smell her *****." I was confused. She was wearing trousers.

After the concert, everyone was waxing lyrical about the concert, whilst he bought himself double JD + Coke. I figured he was just in a bad mood but then he started flirting with the other women in the group. Oh hell no. I pulled him aside for a chat. Turns out that despite everything he'd said, he didn't know how to tell me, so he figured it was easier to show me his lack of interest instead. He'd also become best friends with my ex-friend Tat, who turned out to have a bit of a thing for him too. I've warned you before about watching your single friends, my singirls. Tat had told him about our christening colour scheming three years ahead of schedule. Now he doesn't call me anymore.

A woman's worth is more than a concert ticket, so later that week I reminded him that he still owed me. His response was that he'd bought my friends lots of drinks that night so that should make us even. Bloody accountants with their double book-keeping systems. He eventually apologised for his behaviour that night and he's all loved up now with a kid way before his 40s but to me he was just another of The Crushes.

8. The Boyfriends

These were men I met who claimed at one point or other to be my boyfriend. Or maybe I claimed them as a boyfriend. They were more than flings in my mind and hence were potential partners. To think I was quasi-engaged to one. If he'd actually proposed instead of assuming that I would just marry him who knows where I would be right now? Not writing this book. The boyfriends were pivotal lessons in how vague the term had become and how a boyfriend to me is something that I had in my early 20s but was certainly not what I wanted in my 30s. Oh wait, I'm officially still only 28. Ignore that. As you were my singirls, as you were.

House (Potential) Hubby

One summer I almost emigrated as I attempted to invest in a lifelong property.

Earlier on in the spring, I'd received a friend request from a guy I dated briefly at university. He invited me to Washington DC to come visit him and see if we still connected. An all-expenses paid holiday. They always sounded too good to be true and yet I couldn't say no. I did recall the reason for our first breakup was because he had forgotten to tell me that he was already invested in another property that turned out to be his now ex-wife. I was his holiday home, I guess.

It was a very exciting time for me, and I threw myself into this with my usual gusto. Waxing, facials, more waxing, pedicures, manicures and even *more* waxing. I'm not even hairy and yet I saw more wax in two weeks than I'd ever done before. Thanks to John Lewis I bought all new underwear that matched and accentuated parts other underwear couldn't reach. I designed a wardrobe that could fit into one suitcase for 2 weeks – a black/red mix and match combination. And I got my hair braided. Natural hair is a minefield at the best of times but who knew what humidity issues I would face?

So, I arrived in DC glistening with anticipation and the lack of sleep one can only achieve in economy class. And there he was. And I fell, my singirls. Literally and metaphorically. That suitcase was heavier than I thought. We snogged in the car, shagged all over the apartment and pillow talked every night. It was the perfect holiday and somewhere, over paella, I decided that he was more than just a timeshare. This was a long-term investment.

When I returned to London, I spent hours with my boyfriend on Skype who turned out to be more attentive than any other boyfriend I had ever known. We made the sort of home improvements in weeks that take most folk months. He asked me to move to the States and despite my reservations I said yes. After all this was it, right? There was talk of a future and plans being made.

I told him I would need a while though as my work was here and I wouldn't be able to work there at all initially. He told me that he could take care of me and that I wasn't to worry. My favourite words. He came over to London so that I could show him all that I would be leaving behind, and I was sold. This was it, my singirls – House Hubby Two! The DHL package had been delivered.

Then it was time for my second viewing. I'd fallen in love the first time, but the second visit was all about seeing the flaws and suddenly my DC penthouse appeared to be subsiding. First, he was late to meet me at the airport. Apparently, he'd run out of gas. Then the apartment was filthy as he had forgotten to hire a cleaner like he had the first time. There was no food in the house except for some frozen peas. Why are frozen peas always the last remaining food? Does anyone eat them? Then he had forgotten to book my braiding hair appointment and another potential buyer, his ex-girlfriend, was on the phone every day. There were cracks everywhere. Then the car got clamped due to unpaid tickets and I discovered I was dating a man who hated to be alone and was over $150,000 in student debt.

I panicked. I didn't think I could do poor. I mean at the end of the day without a means for me to work we would be *really* poor. But he calmed me down and explained that he had a plan for paying it back. It wasn't the best of plans, but I was back in the chain. And it was a chain. There was the ex-girlfriend, the ex-wife and many more exes in the picture than even I thought was manageable. This man had a diverse property portfolio whereas I was merely a second-time buyer.

But the worst crime, my singirls, was him forgetting to pay the cable bill. There was me trying to prove to my boss that I could work from overseas. But I couldn't because the internet wasn't working. It turns out that his previous buyer (*aka* ex-girlfriend) had needed to borrow the cable. He was 'broke-broke' and still talking to other potential home buyers? That was it. I pulled out of the sale. On top of that, I never did get my all-expenses trip reimbursed and couldn't even wallow in real life cable films to make myself feel better. His reason for all that cheating was that I was taking too long to close the sale. Now call me a lot of things but slow I am not.

So, with that, I suggest you keep renting, my singirls, 'cos buying is a nightmare in these economic times. And never overstay in what should only ever be a timeshare. You'll never get the time back. You would be better off spending that time in a sounder investment… like yourself.

Happy house hunting!

P.S. House Hubby married a girl from Kenya who only had an inkling of his past indiscretions and moved continents to be with him. She works in finance so hopefully she sorted him out. He called me to gloat about the coming nuptials and I stupidly let him. I asked him to give a prognosis of the marriage and he was confident that her conservatism would bend to his way with time. I reflected on this and I think in all honesty I was just too independent and wilful. She is younger and more malleable so he's probably right. I however see this whole episode as just another example of a LEE – a Lucky Effing Escape.

Ghosting the Wannabes

Do you remember that Matthew McConaughey movie *Ghosts of Girlfriends Past*? I know my precious I too try to forget it. I remember going to the cinema in Spring 2009 and arguing vehemently for it as opposed to some action movie. I won only because I argued that anything Matthew was in had to be halfway decent. I clearly hadn't seen *Fool's Gold* by then.

Anyway a few blogs are on the *Ghosts of my Boyfriends Past*. Those are the ones that just refuse to go away despite my best intentions to eliminate them through meditation and positive mental attitude.

Take The Chef for instance. Not a boyfriend but a snog buddy for one night. As far as I was concerned, we were over when it was clear he lied about his age and put himself as younger than me. He was clearly an uncle. He then proceeded to piss me off by calling at 11.30pm. Yes, I was awake but clearly you think that there was no one else in my bed to be that cocky and call late. Lekky blanky and

I were in, enjoying a juicy romance novel thank you kindly. I got another call from him the following week but I ignored it. I just don't have the energy to tell people about themselves anymore. By people I mean men and by men, I mean the strange men I attract. How is he acting like we are in a relationship?

So, as I made my way back from my early dental appointment where I was told I couldn't eat for two hours afterwards, I figured I better hit the road and do some shopping. This wasn't my best look. I was in the only pair of jeans I own (I don't understand jeans), trainers and my hair wasn't saying much to the world except we weren't that thorough with the comb that morning. So, imagine my horror when I came out of Waitrose waddling with two bags and saw The Chef. He squinted his eyes in a 'do-I-know-you' way and I just looked away. This wasn't going to be easy as I couldn't slip into Bang and Olufsen with so much shopping. I considered my options and figured... I would have to out walk him.

Now, The Chef was tall and had long strides. I'm short and had shopping. But I wasn't going to let this ghost catch me. I did what any self-respecting woman would do in my situation – I power walked the shit out of the Kings Road. I know it would have been easier to confront him and tell him not to call me with his nonsense but there was one thing stopping me. You can't let the last image the person has of you be of you looking rough and shopping. I now will have to meet up with him just to end it when I'm wearing a little black dress.

Hey, I don't make the rules my singirls. I'm just a slave to them. Drat! This means I have to start planning my pop-to-the-shop outfits better.

Chaste Dating

So, although I'm not a fan of American teen movies and worse, anything vampiric, I have to admit that chaste dating, especially in a time of social distancing could be the answer we have all been looking for.

What do I mean? Some of you, and by you, I mean those who have kissed plenty of frogs and froglittas, are tired of dating, or of sleeping with someone too soon and then realising they were a dick or dicklitta. (I sense a theme with my feminising of words which, in a non-binary age, I could just avoid completely but creating new words is kind of fun).

But have we ever given a moment to consider how quickly we jump into having sex? I'm not saying we need to do the Steve Harvey 90 Day Probation or the religious no-sex- before-marriage thing, but we may need a moment's pause before we let yet another person's energy and potential hygiene into our spaces because, the reality is that energy can linger.

My Chaste Dating: Part 1

I've chaste dated twice in my life. I came across one of my old diaries and it turns out that I dated a dude I thought was, and I quote, 'well fit'. Turns out that younger me had a very limited vocabulary.

Well Fit Dude was incredibly shy. He would wear two pairs of trousers because he didn't want his skinny legs on display. On top of that, because he was only able to make a move when he was high on weed and that wasn't sexy, we dated for 100 days with not even so much as a snog. I feel like I should get a refund on my angst years. That's almost a third of a year wasted whilst all my friends were happily bonking half of North West (and West) London.

But I wasn't upset about it. I kind of found the lack of sexual activity a bit of a relief. I don't think skinny legs would have turned me on either and we were very different. He thought the fact that I was studying made me 'well smart.' I learned that there were online qualifications that were basically certificates which were never mentioned by my school's career counsellor.

It was more the lack of communication between us on the subject *and* the peer pressure to shag that annoyed. I realised years later that friends are actually the worst influences on a relationship and should be kept out of them as much as possible. The decision to fuck isn't by committee.

My Chaste Dating: Part 2

This one was more recent. He was younger and something told me to state my intentions to not have sex with him for three months. He accepted this rather quickly which should have told me that our sex drives weren't on the same level. Not even three months later and we had broken up. Do I regret not sleeping with him? Nope. Turned out he had a touch of the depression and lacked motivation to do anything 'relation-shippy' so, we just weren't in the same place at the same time. He also forgot my birthday because he was so excited by the release of *Thor 3* that it erased his mind of the fact that he had a girlfriend. Sex may have made me want to try to fix him, which is a habit I'm trying to break so, big sigh of relief all round.

Anyway, the key to chaste dating is simple. Work out your why. It could be that you just want to be sure before diving into another relationship, have just come out of something heavy or damaging or have health-related issues. There are a lot of reasons, but you need to have a why. State your intentions so both of you agree to the terms. Don't pretend you're about that chaste life then sleep with them on date number four. It's confusing! So here is a little guide:

1. Set a time limit on chasteness or at least a decision on whether you want to continue dating. Nobody likes a timewaster and there's nothing worse than someone stringing you along for months with expensive dates when they know they're never going to go any further. Undercover friend zoning or what. Froglittas, you're particularly notorious for this.

2. Is kissing OK? Oral? Hand holding? Sleepovers? Phone sex? Frottage? Be clear. Don't blur lines and potentially upset someone who didn't understand and agree to your boundaries.

3. Plan stuff to do – I'm writing this during COVID-19 times so this may be watching a movie at the same time from separate houses, but you can watch at the same time if you sync properly. Or introduce them to your favourite music. Now may not be the time to introduce him to your naked lounge dancing but, hey, we are all different.

4. Enjoy it! There is so much more to a relationship than sex. Like watching how he goes through your lockdown food rations or what Netflix suggestions he has come up with.

5. Make sure that you've done all the boring stuff before sex. Conversations about protection don't make for great foreplay so why not have them early?

I know some of you are sceptical but, who knows, you may find you date fewer frogs and those you date last longer.

9. The Lessons Learned

I know I said I wouldn't lecture you or tell you how best to date but I couldn't resist sharing some of the lessons learned and nuggets of wisdom I picked up along the way. The following are a series of blogs I wrote early in my journey as a singirl. Every date was a potential lesson in tolerance levels. I hope these lessons help you as they outline some core dating values that I think we should all have. And there is a prayer or two in there too. These are for the dating gods and to the big man up there – Santa. I need for them to hear my cries. And yes, some may seem a little snobby but my student days are well and truly behind me. I don't think a man should be making me relive those years, do you?

Anyway, here are a series of blogs that illustrate some great lessons learned.

Pay As You Go

OK, another confession time. Hi, my name is Chelsea and... I can no longer date guys with pay as you go (PAYG) phones. It may sound harsh but here's an ABC of why it just doesn't work for me.

Addict

Cubana, Waterloo. My friends and I bump into a cute-ish guy. This was after a long night of flirting with French rugby guys in the same bar. I'm mentally exhausted as a GCSE in French doesn't get you as far as you think. I say cute-ish because skin-tight jeans don't really look good on any man, do they? And imagine what they are doing to his jewels. OK, I think I picked him up so clearly logic had been drowned in mojitos. My memory tells me that he was cute.

We have a conversation the next day and I like that. He's keen but not in that overbearing way that those who can't get a date are. The conversation is short but that's good too, right? The second time he calls, he asks me to call him back as he's low on credit. Still naïve to the PAYG syndrome I agree. He eagerly talks about himself for 45 minutes with hardly a pause while I play free cell on my computer and try to remember what he looks like. I'm sure he's cute.

I tune back in and it dawns on me that every story he tells centres on him being off his face on drugs. Yes indeed, every few lines are about... him doing lines. He claims that he doesn't do it anymore and isn't an addict or anything, but he does seem to talk about it an awful lot. He explains that he's on PAYG because he'd gotten into a lot of trouble with credit cards and that he's now working for an old school friend cash in hand as a labourer. It's hit and miss as to how much he makes mind you, but on a good week when he can be bothered to show up, he makes... £800. I explain that all my money is for my own addictions – chocolate, cocktails and clothes. Not cocks on coke. I thought we had a spiritual mojito connection but clearly our mobile connection was broken.

Bi-Guy

Heaven, Charing Cross. I'm approached by this pretty young thing walking around with his shirt off. He has that 'look-at-me' swagger with an air of faux innocence that I like and the most gorgeous hazel eyes that he uses to stare at you as he speaks. My friends insist he's gay. I ask and he said he's straight. That was good enough for me. It's 3am, I shrug and proceed to engage in some snog action. I know, how old am I?

A few days later he calls asking me to call him back. I know my singirls, but the body! Numerous missed calls later and I'm getting fed up. The final straw is when I get the old 'low on credit, call me now!' text. I quickly dump him by text as I figure this is in a format he understands. Is it so wrong that his phone habits bother me more than his sexuality? I guess not as I never get to see if that swagger was all hips or if he had something to brag about.

Cheap

Benugos, Waterloo is the only clue I have as to who this guy is. I have a few drunken photos on my phone. He calls days later and quickly asks me what network I'm on. He then says that he can't really chat to me anymore because I'm not on his network and his credit is running low. I figure he means that day. I guess our networks are incompatible because it's been four months. Maybe he's waiting for his contract to kick in?

The Lesson: Now you know me, I'm all about the phone foreplay. I love my phone and my service provider loves me for my commitment to their profit margin. So, when a guy won't commit to a contract what are the chances that he will commit to me? I'm not asking for 18 months. Just long enough for a chapter in his autobiography, half his assets or a really good holiday. So, from now on I say no to PAYG. A girl has got to put her stiletto down.

Or maybe I should just accept that I need to avoid Waterloo.

My Not So Funny Valentine

OK so here's the deal. I tend to put a lot of hope and thought into Valentine's Day. Don't ask me wh,y my singirls. Even when I was married, it's not like I got

89

more than the standard card and something functional like a steps video for those wintery nights at home whilst I rushed around looking for five perfect gifts for our five imperfect years together.

But this year, this year is different, because not only am I single for the first time in forever, I'm seeing not one, but two delicious men. Call me greedy but I see it as portfolio diversification and I'm not one to preach but in a financial crisis, a girl has to have options. Dinner options.

The first one, Young Banker, is a hangover from the year before. He's a boy that proudly told me that he was a year older than last year. I'm glad that as a banker he has conquered the concept of counting up. He claims not to be the same cheap, lazy young man who couldn't be bothered to make an effort anymore. I claim to be the same demanding chick who couldn't cook so when he books me a whole nine days before V-Day, I'm almost impressed.

Then he texts me with two hours to go to the meal and asks me if I have any food preferences? A tad late, I think. We meet and make our way to an Asian restaurant called dim t in Pimlico. On the way, we pass a Nando's and he suggests that we go there instead. I tell him firmly that I support Nando's every week and today I want something more romantic.

I think he feels that all his efforts have been spent as we sit to eat a meal where I chat with my friend Sugar on Messenger and he regales me with tales of erm … I really don't remember any of them. I know it's rude, but I'm mildly pissed off. That year hasn't made any difference because he hasn't changed a bit.

At the end of the meal he proudly presents the waitress with his 2-for-1 voucher. She proudly tells him that it doesn't work on the weekends. I reluctantly offer to pay for my share (£17.50) and only his reluctant refusal of my offer wins him a space in the cab back to my place.

Once at home, just as I think things can't get any worse, he jumps onto my laptop and begins to search porn sites. He can't even be bothered to think up his own foreplay. Really? That's it; the boy is shown the door.

Thankfully, Valentine's Day is saved by Guy Two who accidentally sent my card to the address upstairs. A few days later, it finally makes its way downstairs (but I can feel my neighbour's resentment steaming off the envelope she'd tried to hastily stick back together).

He then buys me chocolates, perfume and knickers. Now you know that red isn't my colour but when a man asks you to wear the gift for him, what's one to do but buy a pair of matching red heels and fishnet stockings?

The Lesson: Putting all your faith into one day isn't necessarily the way to go. Every year I think that men are going to get it right. They oh so often don't though. It's their way of retaining masculinity and control by messing up on something that is irrationally important to us. So now I always have two options because a girl has so few pleasures in life. It may as well be as close to guaranteed on Valentine's Day as possible.

My Alternative Girlfriend

Keep this between us but... I had to go on the run at one point. Not from the law or amazingly, not from a man. No, I was officially in a relationship... with another girl. It can take a while for you to realise that you are involved. Their tactics are so stealthy and subtle that MI5 should recruit them. It's only when they decide to date you without your permission that you'll know.

Mine started off innocently enough. We met and she seemed like a sociable happy-go-lucky type of sister with 'a life'. She was a little more conservative than me and was slightly determined and dreamy-eyed about meeting a guy called The One but showed no other signs.

Then, one day, I got a mysterious call from her out of the blue saying she wanted to 'hang out'. She needed a 'friendly' ear. I barely knew her. Surely, I wasn't the 'friend' she was referring to? At this point I should have probed. Why didn't I probe? Instead I envisaged a passion fruit mojito and chocolate brownies from Bar Ha Ha and ignored the danger signs.

Eight hours later and my life had changed irrevocably. For hours I sat through this woman's analysis of every single break up from the age of 16 and where things went wrong. I tried to be understanding, sympathetic and caring but I kept thinking, Why is she talking to me about all of this? Why aren't we talking about me?!

The trouble is that I could really see why the men in her life needed a break from her... a permanent break. I couldn't cope with that level of intensity even with alcohol to distract me, let alone sober trying to watch Match of the Day. This is the only time I have sympathised with the other side. You had to love her though because she was an eternal optimist who believed that one day, she would meet The One and live happily ever after.

But then there were the late-night calls of woe, the requests for 'crazy' girls' nights out that turned into therapy sessions with the constant analysis of 'where-are-all-the-good-black-men'. She must have been crazy to ask me because if I knew I wouldn't have been sitting at home on my computer chatting to her.

So now I'm on the run. It's ruining my social life as I avoid being online. Does this woman never sleep? She thinks I work half the week in Scotland and that I barely go out. I can't post pictures on Facebook. It's no way to live.

Funnily enough, her number is withheld so she corners me when I assume it's a recruitment consultant. It's always the same theme with a teary end. She's single and she doesn't want to be. I, on the other hand, was only just beginning to enjoy being single again. I had accepted that there was a lot of research I had to do before I settled again. Yes, it was on.

The Lesson: Take care my singirls, as this species is growing and on the loose. Hmm... methinks my plans for a career change to life coaching might have to be put on hold. Hang on, there's more.

Some Lessons for the Blokes

Along the way, I have picked up some lessons that I think the men in our lives should learn too. It's only fair that I share these because after all we are in this together... and perhaps, it they learn a thing or two, this whole dating thing might be a little bit easier for us singirls...

When a Woman Pays the Bill

Remember the dating recession of 2010-14? Yes, I've tried to block most of it out of my mind too because, those were some dark and harrowing times. As much as I love my Nando's, nobody wants to be eating it two to three times a week because of... budget. But luckily as the new year broke so did those times. Thank you, black men of London, for letting go of Nando's. Now we can resume business as usual which means the awkward question of who pays the bill comes up. Nobody has a loyalty card with a whole chicken on it.

Traditionally I would say the person that asks, the bloke or going Dutch are the only answers, but there is a new phenomenon creeping into our lives that needs to be explained. When she pays the bill. It can mean one of only three things.

1. She thinks you can't afford to pay

Talk about the recession, say you live with your parents in your 40s or talk about how hard it is to be an artist in this world where your art is too *avant garde* to sell (you draw. It's comic books. It's hardly post-modern or *avant garde* but, OK), and the chances are she's going to dry up and take pity on you instead. Yes, she'll make the right noises and try to save you from what is fast becoming a pathetic picture, but would she want to have sex with that? You've friend-zoned yourself. And if she does want to take all of that, there is some co-dependency crap in her past that will rear its ugly head later. Ultimately you may be thinking it's a nice gesture but that's not for first dates. Save that for later.

2. She never wants to see you again

You pissed her off. She may be too polite to show it, but this woman doesn't like you at all. So, she's making sure that she's free of you forever. As the not so late and not so great boy band Bros sang, 'I Owe You Nothing'. This woman wants to be able to leave this scenario without guilt. She basically has written you off as a friend, fuck buddy or potential partner. Take it gracefully and accept that she was nice enough to end it without the nice guy BS that so many throw in there at the end. None of us need more male friends. This is a misconception that must die. I already have my five. No vacancies left.

3. She's more alpha than you

The most dangerous is the woman that feels the need to show you that she doesn't need you and can take care of herself. Whilst I believe in independence, some take it too far. Let him be chivalrous if that is who he is but don't push it. I remember bumping into a cutie on the way back from the supermarket who tried to chat me up for four blocks but watched me carry my bags all that way? Couldn't he see I was struggling? But I digress. The real issue is that she still has some work to do or is looking for a man she can dominate. Either way this is not necessarily a good trait. Tread with caution.

PS – I know this is advice for the men, but I must have a moan about those guys that forget their wallets. In this day and age there is no excuse. He can pay by PayPal or online. Nonsense. Don't fall for it my precious. Grab your purse and run. Don't feel shamed into paying his way. Especially not at Michelin-star restaurants you didn't suggest. The fuckery is real.

Right, I'm off to look for affordable restaurants for the future. Always be prepared I say. And OpenTable. They are your friend.

10. Words of Advice

*I*gnore these at your peril. It took me a while to learn that men drop clues about their personalities in the kind of porn they watch, female friends are now your competition and Santa doesn't always hear your prayers. As with all prayers you have to be really specific about the kind of guy you ask for.

The Porn Files

So, you think you're adventurous with your one Ann Summers vibrator and a few raunchy novels? Well my singirls, no matter how happy a man is, he has a history. A porn history and this is the file you need to tap into. Forget the ex-file. That one is simple. He couldn't/wouldn't commit. She flipped after four years and slashed his tyres/football shirts/music collection/credit rating. Yep, we've all been there. The real drama is porn.

Now you're thinking, 'Not my man, I give him everything he wants and more.' No, you don't, you smug cow. Most men desire more than matching undies, a blindfold, handcuffs and some chocolate body paint. Don't ask. Needless to say, the sheets didn't survive.

The first trick is to gain access then quickly locate the heart of the man, the private collection. Send him out for some tampons then check everywhere including his internet history. Assume every man has porn and look for worrying signs of sex practices you'd steer well clear of when you're drunk. Hey, if double anal penetration is your bag then go forth with glee (and generous lashings of lube). If you're more the 'blow job on his birthday' type then make a plan to extricate yourself pretty quickly – but only after sex because you never know my singirls, with the right man at the helm you may find yourself enjoying it. Don't ask. I just can't tell you.

Let's not be judgmental now. Fantasies are a deep-rooted thing based on early sexual experiences. He's into *Big Jugs Weekly* because his first teacher had big jugs and didn't wear a bra. Well, I guess they're not that complex after all. Then again, I turned down a guy in a Soho sex shop who had been flirting a bit too hard with the blow-up dolls. We all have our limits.

If you can't find his stash, then ask. Be careful, they're getting sneakier. My ex had all his porn on his computer as password-protected downloads. He put up 15 minutes of resistance before I endured a long night of badly shot black porn. You know, with shots of the director's friends in the background eating chicken? It got so dire that I pretended to be just as turned on by the mother/daughter/boyfriend scene just so that I could seduce him in time to watch *Project Runway*. It wasn't even the final and I'm not that into fashion.

But know that this isn't about him. It's about us making a choice. I know a girl who broke up with her partner recently after he made her watch his favourite film, *The Secretary*. I heard this and thought this made him slightly quirky and open-minded. She saw it as signs of a controlling, obsessive nature

98

with masochistic undertones. So, you see how important the porn files are. Open them!

Hmm, I wonder if it's too soon to ask her for his number.

Hold It In

So, I have a new theory on getting a man that's so simple even I can follow it. As soon as you spot a potential SLS (shag/life-partner/sperm donor) do not leave him unattended for a second. Ever. Especially with your friends. I don't care if you need to pee. Hold It In! You're really thirsty? Be a tough cookie and send a friend to the bar. Your make-up needs attention? No girl should be wearing that much MAC anyway – yes you!

One night I'd just announced my latest romance to everyone. The signs were good. Physical attraction, all day communication and he'd even mentioned the C word first. Yep, that's right. Children! I in turn didn't mention that I had their names picked out and was actively looking at wedding dresses and schools. See, it was the perfect relationship.

So, a group of us met up in Moonlighting, Soho (don't ask) and my good friend warned me to tread cautiously. At the time I was grateful because it's nice when someone else has your back.

A few weeks later at Brown Sugar and the dynamics had shifted. I'm left watching their intense sexual chemistry wondering what I'm going to do with those hastily purchased wedding expo tickets. I cursed the night I let them catch the night bus together. So, you see, the only back she was interested in was hers and getting on it. Meow.

Then on a recent group holiday to Rome I bumped into this guy outside a bar, Anima. He was the best person to explore the nightlife in Rome with. A real bar-fly just like yours truly. Well that was it my singirls, I was hooked. I introduced him to the rest of the group (mistake *numero uno*) and got my flirt on. But then, the club got fuller and afraid of the dreaded glisten/sweat natural hair effect I rushed to the busy bar to get some water (mistake *numero duo*). Twenty minutes later, I stumble back, hair a mess, only slightly refreshed to find him slow dancing with my friend to the latest Justin Timberlake club track. I now hate JT. On top of that, I was left chatting to the strange friend obsessed with pizza-making techniques. I asked if he'd ever heard of Domino's. Not surprisingly as an Italian he didn't seem to get pizza humour.

At our age, be sure that whoever it is you have your eye on, your friends will have spotted them too. Yes, your shy, quiet girlfriend who is supposedly still so into her ex is now your potential SLS's girlfriend. Oh, they will plead their innocence as they are walking down the aisle. And you? You're the bridesmaid with the too bright smile or the godmother to a child that screams when you hold her because she knows what really went down that night.

So, my theory is simple – when it comes to who will get the man it's about who can hold it in the longest. So, flex those muscles my singirls. You never know, it might just help you keep the man too.

My Christmas Prayer

Every year it's the same. Every year without fail I start praying. I send a prayer to the big guy upstairs asking for a man who will treat me like a queen, spoil me like a princess and never ever question my need to buy shoes, or eat chocolate and drink cocktails before afternoon tea. It's not too much to ask for, is it?

And yet every year Santa says the same ole thing. No. Well, I'm tired of listening to the cuddly guy in the ill-fitting crushed velvet suit. So, this year my singirls, well, you know *moi*, this year I had a plan. I was going to find my own man. You know – a gift to me.

And I made some headway. By August I'd successfully stopped contact with all lovers and 'accidental' friends (cyber lovers, drunken dials and Facebook flirts don't count). January had seen my dalliance with Not So Bachelor Number One who was separated but still living with his wife. He didn't mind practicing kissing under the mistletoe when we were tipsy but when sober he reminded me that he didn't plan to marry until he was 40. He'd just turned 33. Next!

Step forward Bachelor Number Two – Mr April. Own business, serious and cute. We spent a lot of time texting. He gave great text. Who could want more? Apparently, me. On our first date he failed to turn up. Assuming (or kind of hoping) he'd been in an accident, I found out that he was no longer able to dial out, pick up or text. Turns out that he was already giving great text and sex... to his wife. I'm hoping she gave him the gift of breaking the bones in his hands.

Bachelor Number Three was Mr August. Yes, my singirls, I'd almost convinced my mother that this could be the one. He's fertile (has kids), with a hectic job (money and no time to monitor how I spend it) and no wife (and therefore potential boyfriend material). She asked me to send her a picture of him, which I did. She then asked me to send me pictures of alternative sperm donors. He clearly clashed with the theme of her Christmas card photograph. He was no oil painting I will admit. In the end, it was a no from the fussy Mum judge.

Now it's December and I'm back to being realistic and circling the Tiffany catalogue. I just pray for the energy and patience to go on blind dates, flirt online and worse, pretend that I too want to eventually move to Nigeria and build an import business from scratch. I don't, by the way. That would have to be one bloody big diamond to get me out of London.

So, what to do my singirls? Let's drink, be merry and enjoy the fact that only us single girls can get away with truly misbehaving this time of year. We can carry lots of mistletoe, sing bad karaoke and make sure we're standing next to true potential at midnight on New Year's Eve. This, I fear, is as much planning as a single girl can do.

And when you are filling my stocking please slip a few condoms in there for me. I think it's time to find some new lovers to see me through the misery that is an English January.

Where to Find the Men in London

I'm constantly asked where to find black men in London. If I knew I wouldn't be single I retort snidely but then one night… I found the Mecca. It's only taken ten years of looking, an exhausted Oyster card and more dating disaster tales than any one woman should be able to own. I would normally tell you 'Sarf' London as it avoids the metrosexual bougie-ness of both East and West Londonese men but the men in 'Sarf' aren't always as assertive as one would like. I think 'Norf' may have it.

But wait, let me go back. My friend T was having birthday celebrations and suggested Bar 300 in Walthamstow. I know my precious, my Zone 1 radar went off but, I love T, so I decided to make a weekend of it and stay at Mama Black's nearby. Yes, I know that Walthamstow is only 25 mins from Victoria but I'm really not one for travelling across the city solo late at night.

Typically, I arrived before the others and settled myself in with Prosecco. Note to the management, the Martini Prosecco is not the one. I beg you review your choice. It was quiet and I was already fantasizing about heading out early to catch the last few recorded *Big Bang Theory* episodes with my mum. Then I spotted him. A staring short dude with a vapour cigarette and the angst-ridden face of someone who wasn't happy to be there. Later he came up to stand behind me but still didn't say anything. As he left the bar he came up, mumbled a compliment then ran away. Not the reaction I expected.

Then there was the Polish guy who said he came with a friend, but the friend had to leave early to take his kids to football the next day... this is a small bar, dude. I never saw you with anyone else.

Then there was the promoter who lied and said he was having his birthday party the following week and he wanted to give me a flier but he couldn't let anyone else see. He looked around feverishly as we talked. Was he being watched by the Po Po? Why can't he just be honest and say he was there with a woman. But no, we did some drug exchange handshake for said flier. I looked at it this morning and... Ilford? He's having a laugh. Nah mate. I'm not about to call.

My favourite was the 55-year-old who didn't work because he owned lots and lots of property but thought that Chelsea was too posh an area and that I was too young for him. I promptly agreed that he was too old for me and that my area was just fine, thanks. He asked for my number and I said no as I didn't want to lead him on. So then as he left with his band of fellow retired men (none of them were under 60, I kid you not) he slipped me his business card. Reminds me, I must get some dating business cards made up. It seems to be the new networking technique in bars and clubs. I also have to practise the discrete handshake so as not to be observed by anyone else, hence allowing me the opportunity to give out cards to everyone!

I came home with two numbers I didn't want and sore feet from the dancing. Aside from the hour-long reggae portion then rare grooves for an hour the music was on point. As I told 55-year-old, I'm too young to remember '80s clubbing days. I was watching *Top of The Pops*.

Happy Hunting!

11. The Crossroads

So, as you can see, I haven't really gotten a handle on this dating thing. I've learned a few lessons yes, like the importance of knowing what I like, not crushing on those that don't deserve it and that PAYG is not for me. But I didn't feel like I had a plan yet.

Let's go back. When I wanted to get married, I had a plan. A plan of how my life with my husband was going to include a house in Hillingdon, four brats and a wonderful career as something fabulous, which meant that I would travel lots but not too far so as not to be able to be a good mother. I'd watched *Wife Swap* and seen the guilt those poor working mothers endured. So I had a plan and aside from work which was going really well, the rest of the plan hadn't really manifested. Since the marriage, I'd bounced from one man to the next but nothing apart from potential House Hubby had stuck. So, I realised that I needed to figure out what I wanted if this was going to give me the family I dreamt of. I needed a plan B.

My thing was this. Dating again was highlighting the things that I liked and the things that I didn't. Initially it wasn't easy for me to tell the guy that I didn't like something. I didn't want to come across as if I was still in a naggy-wife mode and I wanted to avoid those sorts of accusations. So instead I just let him do what he wanted then reviewed it afterwards. It wasn't healthy but it was what it was.

But then it struck me that I didn't really want a relationship just yet. I actually wanted to enjoy myself and my new-found freedom. Figure out who the older Chelsea was because I wasn't the same person as I had been coming fresh out of university. I needed a new plan. A plan for fun maybe?

Dear Santa

Now, I know, (like lots of men) when I talk, you sometimes don't hear everything I say, but please, after last year's Christmas prayer, I really feel that I'm going to have to be a bit more specific if we're going to crack this second-husband wish.

I know that you are busy Santa and that there are too many women out there in the same boat as me but to be perfectly honest, I think with a little Chelsea teamwork we can crack this thing by Valentine's Day. So here is my Santa gift wish list for the coming year:

Single

I really am not one to share. When one guy proposed to someone else just two weeks after we broke up, I realised that he'd been a timeshare. It's also bad that I have accidentally dated married men. Santa dear, can't you mark them? Maybe a partridge tattoo on their neck? I might be regularly merry, but I'm not ready to be any man's ho ho ho.

Ambitious

Oh Santa. Bartenders and students are great but it's not so much fun when they are over 30, eyeing up your flat as if it were their new home but still on a PAYG contract. I don't need a professional man, but, seriously, someone who can't get a mobile contract is just not on. Please sprinkle some tinsel their way and give them the gift of wanting to be the best that they can be. If I have to sit through another old homemade rap/band CD, I think I might be spending New Year's behind bars for assault.

Nubian

I know it doesn't snow much in Africa but I would still like an African diaspora Nubian elf to... help me fill my stockings. A prince please Santa. None of this nonsense where you send me visa hunters. It's cheating.

Trained

I really thought you had it when you brought me the divorcé. On Skype it was hot, exciting and I almost believed that I heard angels sing. Hark! On dates he was constantly late and made love like an over eager adolescent. I was bruised by his clumsy attempts and nursed bite marks for three weeks afterwards. I don't mind tweaking Santa, but he needs to know how to make the angel on the top of the tree light up. At 40, surely, he should be trained by now.

Accessible

Don't get me wrong my Santa, I've had real moments of fun this year, but it has nearly all been on the internet with men on other continents. Please can you sleigh some of those fine men over here? I will gladly pass the gift of cybersex on.

There are obviously other things I want, such as good health, wealth and for the annoying woman at work to get sacked, but we can focus on those separately (please see special envelope attached and marked Private and Confidential with Appendices A to G). So, to all the single belles out there: Merry Christmas my singirls as we try to find our very own Mr Jingle.

Plan B

Plan B wasn't what I was expecting. Up to this point I was looking for FuHu. I didn't think I wanted to be single. But then I realised a few things:

1. I was starting to enjoy being single.
2. I hadn't quite mastered the science of internet dating. I was sure my luck lay there.
3. I wasn't sure that I was ready for FuHu, as emotionally I wasn't there.
4. I needed to get myself some new friends as my current ones were all coupled up and constantly avoiding me or encouraging me to find The One or Theo Neman as I call him.

I made my own plans. I decided that I needed a dating detox. I was making schoolgirl errors because the game and I had changed, but not in the same direction.

I decided to make some time to catch up. Instead of rushing into another bad relationship, I needed instead a year that was completely about me and getting back in touch with who I was and what I wanted out of life. Of course, I still wanted a partner and kids eventually but did I want them immediately? Was I just competing with my ex-husband who had managed to get himself remarried at miraculous speed? It was time to get my plan B together and so it was with this that I went to a place in Brixton called Plan B where my dating research began.

PART 2

Dating Research

So, this was it my singirls, a new start. I was going to date for fun and not for FuHu. But something told me that even with my newfound resolve it wasn't going to be as simple as I'd hoped. Surely there couldn't be that many men out there who would just be up for fun with no strings attached? Well, it was time to find out. I had to venture into a world I still knew so little about and just hope for the best… hope that I found my Hubby Number 2.

12. Friends and Food

The Diet

*D*uring this time, I began to train for a marathon, so I was put on a diet to maximise my energy and muscle power. I say a marathon like there was ever going to be more than one which, as I can tell you now will never be the case. I completed the marathon in just over 5 hours which is rubbish but that's one more thing that is ticked off the bucket list, I guess. Note to self, the reason people don't do marathons more often is because after 2 hours of running, you are pretty bored of people wrapped warmly giving out jelly babies and shouting encouragement at you. OK I wasn't tired of the jelly babies, but I was tired of the, "Come on Chelsea! You can do it!" I know I can. I just didn't want to do it that much without some union breaks. Marathon organisers: champagne pit stops are an option not explored in my opinion.

What I found however is that this new diet and exercise regime made me… horny. I wanted sex and I wanted it often. Luckily, I have men around me who were happy to oblige and when I couldn't find them, I soon discovered there were options on the internet.

Here is my thing. I hate diets with a passion. Anything which denies me the pleasure of carbs and chocolate and champagne won't work for me. I also hate cold food. I need food that warms me. Denying me food was not really working for me. I'm also allergic to the gym. Everything from having to exercise during certain hours, to the group of unemployed guys who *always* hog the weights, to the skinny women in matching kit, to having to shower in a communal space just seems wrong to me. But running three times a week? I could do that. And I did get to a weight I thought I would never see again. In fact, during the marathon I sweated out 3lbs of water and finally reached my self-imposed target weight.

And so that is what I did, and I've maintained a fighting fit weight ever since. I slip on the exercise and I have to cut down on the Haribos every now and again but that's winter. Spring comes around and I don't mind doing a 10K for the sake of my sex drive and stamina. Both are important my singirls. And it's great for your mental health too. Here's to diets that don't deny you chocolate!

P.S. I've since discovered that I'm lactose intolerant, have a low immune system which hates acidic imbalances and adult eczema. Chocolate has not been the same. Instead I'm combining raw food with low red meat and low carbs in an attempt to manage what exercise won't. Wish me luck my singirls. I have a feeling I'll be falling off this wagon often before I get it right.

The Wanker

I have met some interesting characters. Some cute, others weird and some so scary that I have their details in a file called Missing, in case I ever go missing. Please my singirls review this file carefully and submit to the appropriate authorities if ever you lose me.

One of these characters was a guy called The Wanker. Not his birth name admittedly, he was a Caribbean-born male – I will not name the island for fear of giving it an unwarranted bad rep – with a beautiful lilting accent and the frame of a sprinter. Well he would have done if he hadn't eaten his way through the pie shop. But there was something sweet about him. We met on a dating site and initially he pretended to want a relationship but after I made it clear we weren't a match, he opened up about his... needs.

Working late nights at hotels can be very dull. The Wanker used the time effectively to chat to random strangers online including me. On nights off he could be found travelling to exotic places like Luton and Kent for sex. But sadly, for The Wanker he was no oil painting. Once, he told me, he spent all night talking to a woman who invited him to Luton for a hot and heavy session. He arrived at the woman's house; she took one peek out of the window, gasped and promptly switched off all the lights and pretended not to be home. That was one long frustrating drive back to South London for The Wanker.

Between wanks we would talk. He'd been single for a while and being new to the country didn't have a wide circle of friends and family. He was a sweetheart, bless him, but something told me that we weren't a match. But he did love to wank off and talk dirty. It was not to the sound of my voice thankfully but to the sound of his own. He would sit there and tell me what he was going to do to me when he saw me and then, all too soon it would be over.

I had my script. I sat at home giving myself a pedicure and moaned at the appropriate places with 'Oooh yeah, yeah baby'. Little did he know, I was talking to the Haribos. You know the jelly baby ones in the Supermix. Then he would cum, thank me politely and tell me about his latest aborted attempt to meet up with some woman from the internet. He wasn't having much luck. Then he offered to come to visit me one night but I wasn't having it. My bed was assembled by my own fair hands and I don't think it would have taken his weight. I'm many things, my singirls, but a DIY expert or pity shagger I am not.

I soon tired of The Wanker. Mainly because there is only so much pleasure that I can get from listening to the fantasies of a guy who was struggling to transition from the virtual to real life. I also found it really tiring trying to think up different ways to feign interest and fake an orgasm. I wasn't really inspired and drama wasn't my strongest subject at school. Besides, I believe an orgasm is only as good as the person giving it to you.

However, it helped improve my phone sex and I learned that for some there is satisfaction in just being heard. It did make me wonder about all those men out there on night shifts using their time to chat to strangers online with no real desire to ever get into a relationship. Now when I see security guards, I give them an extra nice smile out of sympathy. But, no more wankers for me, my singirls. I'm just not built for aural stimulation.

Running in Heels

Sometimes we go through things that teach us lessons and remind us of who our friends are. Mine came after a Whitney Houston concert. Already low, I listened to my iPod whilst humming badly to Bobby Mcferrin's 'Common Threads' as one often does. This is not a happy song. It's a haunting, slightly worrying ditty that I first came across on that Alaskan programme *Northern Exposure* and I did think initially that it was an indigenous Indian song. But somehow, I still love it and as I walked along, I enjoyed the comforting sound of my heels on the pavement – I'm not light footed, believe you me.

I was making the short walk from the Kings Road to my place when I felt a sharp pain on my butt and my headphones were jerked from my ears. You have to kick me pretty hard on the butt for me to feel it, as testified by the bruise that came up only three days later. I turned around and there were two young women standing there looking at me strangely. I noticed that one of them had wet, red hair and assumed that she was bleeding. OMG had she been attacked? The poor thing!

Yes, my singirls, I seriously hadn't realised that I was being mugged and instead asked if *they* were OK. Turns out the blood was… cheap, wet hair dye. It was a bad fashion mistake fuelled by copious amounts of drugs and alcohol. They were both high as kites and they had left the hair wet because they wanted my hard-earned cash for more. Err, I didn't think so.

The small one made another grab for my bag and my instincts kicked in. Forget the judo lessons, I hit her around the head with the bag which thankfully had half my entire belongings in it and gathered useful evidence as said bag was covered in the wet hair dye. She tried to grab the iPod again and I held on for dear life. Bless, I may have just given it to her but a), she didn't realise that it was only an iPod shuffle and b), something told me she wouldn't have appreciated the intricate sounds of Bobby McFerrin.

Then the other one smashed a bottle on the ground, and I thought to myself, err, why am I standing here fighting two women? And in heels I'd worn all day? If I didn't die now, then my ancestors would surely kill me for such stupidity. Besides I'm not one of those girls that could carry off a facial scar that would evoke men to feel protective of me. This was one of those classic grab-your-bag-and-run situations. So, I ran looking like a demented 100m drag queen sprinter, reached home and called the Po Po. And now for a rare shout out to the K&C police. They were round in 15 minutes, had caught the girls 15 minutes later and had a statement from me in under an hour. The seven police cars and ambulance were a tad overkill but… I felt special. They treated this like a drill. You passed with flying colours Kensington and Chelsea police! You can tell Victim Support to take me off the list now though.

Anyway, clearly shaken, I called my male friend who had been at the concert with me. I thought about it but didn't call Mama Black as she would have thrown dramatics before threatening to plot vengeance on all burgundy-haired girls in the hood for touching her baby. But my friend's initial cursory response was to ask if I was OK then say, "I know this is wrong but, is Lottie OK?"

Who is Lottie you ask? Yes, that's what I was thinking. This was the other friend at the concert who he had a massive crush on. He had met her all of twice up till that day. Lottie is the girl that has some sort of special milk shake juju that brings all the boys to the yard. Her milk is better than mine. Apparently, she hadn't texted him to say she'd arrived home safely and given him the opportunity he so craved to initiate some well thought out banter. My moment of being vulnerable and needy was ruined by his cock getting in the way? To be clear Lottie and I lived in opposite directions so how I would know how she was doing was beyond my comprehension. And why ask if you know it's wrong? I gave him a good piece of my mind in between Po Po visits and statements.

Eventually my dramatic reaction to his question (apparently, I'm more like my Mum than I think) provoked two responses. Over the subsequent weeks it emerged that he thought I was too incredibly sensitive and that I fancied him. Why oh, why do men always think any display of emotion mean you want to f**k them or make them your husband? Didn't he realise that his actions highlighted his lack of protective instincts for me and therefore was an instant turn off? Apparently not, as he continuously dropped vague hints about me liking him for another several weeks. As for me being too sensitive, I am a woman. It's my right to react emotionally to any situation I deem to be emotional. I can't explain it better than that, but all women abide by this rule.

And so, this is what I remember most about the mugging. Not the strung-out druggie girls but the 'friend' who couldn't even be bothered to show sufficient concern. Instead he waited at home for a text that never came from Lottie. Things have never been the same since. As for me, I'm OK really but I've never been able to listen to Bobby without thinking... heels aren't great shoes to escape in. I'm putting flat shoes in my bag as I write this.

P.S. I'm not able to listen to Bobby without flashbacks. McFerrin that is, not Bobby Brown.

Dial Detox

Whilst everyone is on a diet or detox programme to celebrate the new year, I had a different sort of clear out. Yes, my precious, the home could do with a declutter but I'm talking about a virtual one. A dial detox. Anything to avoid cleaning.

I recently tried to block someone on my phone only to find that I'd run out of blocks again! Between car accident and PPI (payment protection insurance – as if you didn't know) cold calls, those website dudes from India (thanks for nothing GoDaddy) and ghosts from a Tinder/PoF past I had more than 600 contacts in my phone. It was time to cull.

I realised that the majority of slide backs happen when drunk with phone in hand and when I was bored with more than a 20-minute cab journey to endure. I scrolled through the names and a lot of names didn't ring any bells or I hadn't heard from aside from one call. It wasn't worth the block.

Besides, a block is not enough. You have to totally delete these people from your life. From your contacts, WhatsApp, email, social media etc. It can take time but it's also time to lose some excess baggage and start screening your calls

The first step was to get rid of any names I didn't recognise. Many more were frenemies who never ever reached out and yet I ran the risk of accidentally butt dialling and a forced conversation. I got rid of anyone with a Plenty of Fish or Tinder in their names too. Jeez, I'd spoken to a lot of wastemen in my time.

Down by more than 50% I was faced with the tricky, emotional exes. Please note that exes may or may not have been actual partners. In these modern times many are timewasters or wastemen who love to hone their skills. I found these to be the hardest ones to let go of at one point as I love a heads up on their fuckeries. But the speed of the delete showed me that they held no real power over my emotions (or their own in some cases). All were permutations of the following:

1. Idiot
2. Prick
3. Prick Do Not Answer (DNA)
4. Dunno
5. Last minute dude from brown sugar
6. The one with the bandanna
7. Talks a lot /is moany/will want money

That was another 20 (OK, 30) easily gone and my phone felt lighter already. My new rule was that if I don't recognise the number because it's not in my phone then Giff Gaff voicemail will have to catch it. Besides most of my exes were way too lazy to actually call me. They preferred the WhatsApp and sneakiness of a message rather than catching me in one of my moods, i.e., not in the mood for them.

The final action was to call those friends I'd missed over the Xmas period. So that took up half an evening. And it was positive. Finally, an opportunity to talk to people who understood the ramifications of a hard Brexit and weren't looking for sex or money! It's therapeutic and you realise how much crap is in your phone.

Next stop: Unsubscribing from all those random emails I never signed up for. Yay!

The Gift Gap

I still feel a little queasy when I recall the moment of shame with amazing clarity. You know how it is my precious when you become friends with a guy and quickly they seep into every part of your life? They have your email, phone number, are connected on Facebook etc., and are the first person you call when your ceiling falls through. He was my ceiling guy. Yes, I knew he had a long distance girlfriend, but she was barely mentioned. So, despite knowing better, I woke up one day and decided... I was in crush. For those of you who know me you will know that this is a regular occurrence and that crushes rain as freely as chocolate and cocktails in my world. It's the perfect love without responsibility but lashings of guilt.

Not being a boyfriend stealer, I kept it to myself but slowly it SEEMED that the feelings were being reciprocated. I saw him more than three times a week at worst and stopped dating. Ok when I say stopped dating, I mean stopped dating new people. I had long standing commitments to maintain!

But as Christmas approached the question of the gift came up. I noticed that he didn't have a man bag so carefully researched the perfect one. I marched up to Peter Jones and confidently purchased it. Then, later that day, he casually mentioned how he hated pretentious man bags and the brand I had just bought. That could explain why he didn't have one.

So, then I was stuck. What to get the man who has and can afford anything? I know he loved to travel and a few months earlier he had mentioned his favourite hotel being in Paris so, I emailed his best friend who dislikes me at the best of times, and he gave me the hotel name. Then I carefully extracted some GCSE French from the internet and planned a call to the hotel to book a lunch. It turns out that they could speak perfect English and didn't need my grammatically incorrect stammering. Eurostar was next and I figured why not make it a group trip and invited the crew who were more than happy for a day trip to Paris.

Meanwhile, he was planning his own surprise and just before the trip he showered me with gifts. Breath mints and a key ring. After carrying out a poll of friends and family I realised that it wasn't my breath that stunk. It was his gifts which reeked of the airport purchases on his last trip to see... his girlfriend.

Gulping down my disappointment, I smiled but inside, my precious, I knew that a man that didn't know that no gift is better than airport gifts (excluding duty free alcohol of course) is not the man for me. So, we went to Paris and had a nice time but there's something about Paris that now leaves a bitter taste in my mouth.

Breath mint anyone?

13. Friends With Benefits

The Grill Guy

I was out one night with friends celebrating my cousin's birthday. For some strange reason I was having a Mary Quant week and turned up in a '60s psychedelic chick dress, boots and a cropped red wig.

I stood out. The thing with birthday parties on a Friday is that some people feel the need to invite the dry people from work. This was one of those parties. I soon started making noises about having to leave as the full effect of my ensemble wasn't being appreciated. As we left, the barman gave me a look and... I told my friends that surely, we could stay for one more drink. I spoke to him and it became apparent that he wasn't the best barman I'd ever met. Two minutes later, he had my number though we were leaving. I'm nothing if not efficient, my singirls. I gave up on being coy a long time ago.

Later that night, I was heading home alone when I got a text from the barman. He was getting on his motorbike and wanted to pass by. At nearly 3am? What kind of girl did he think I was? I needed at least 30 minutes to clean that flat. So, I told him 3.30 and texted him my address.

Quickly, I did the single girl clean. Throw everything in wardrobes, drawers and the spare room and shut the door on that mess. I brushed my teeth, threw on my visitor negligee and walked casually into a spray of perfume. You know how you do. That onesie was hidden well away.

The knock came and as I opened the door smiling, he smiled back. Was that a gold grill in his mouth! Oh dear God. How could I extricate myself from this horror show at 3.30am?

He came in, took out the grill and told me that when he wasn't being an inefficient barman, he was an American wannabe rapper. This wasn't looking good. He was older than me and still wanting to make it as a rapper. He gave me his rap name and a sample of his lyrical tongue. I told him I could think of much better things he could use that tongue for and we soon got down to making music.

A couple of late-night drive-bys later we were lying post-coital and he brought up kids. I told him eventually I would want some but for now I was just happy exploring. He told me that he really wanted kids and that if I was ever pregnant, I could just give him the kid and he would look after it. Assuming this was a naïve comment, I figured it was time that I showed him where I kept the condoms just in case he forgot to bring his own. But then it got me thinking. Who was this guy to whom I was entrusting my most prized possession? My time.

There comes a time when the post-coital conversation turns to work and so he told me about his rap exploits. I didn't know all the artists he mentioned but I knew that I was meant to be impressed. So, weeks later we were still shagging,

122

and I decided that my only option was to investigate this hip-hop thing myself. I typed in his rap name and nothing came up. Maybe he wasn't that successful. So, I typed in his real name.

When the only thing that came up mentioned him being found guilty for third degree larceny, I began to worry. He wasn't even American as the report said he was being deported. I had to look up larceny. This was turning into a crime scene investigation research project.

So, I did what any self-respecting woman would do. I shagged him one last time, gave him a proper grilling and kicked him to the curb. What can I say, his tongue had some uses but Google doesn't lie.

The Gym Giant

We met at an event I was running. Don't ask me why, but he was standing on the side determined not to enjoy himself or crack a smile and I saw a challenge. Luckily for me the dress I wore decided that buttons were an inconvenience and lost themselves as I sashayed over. He gave me that wary look. I was a woman who was going to take away his much-treasured grumpiness and make him have a conversation in a bar. But no, I introduced him and his friend to some women and sauntered off to spread magic and vodka cranberry over the other guests. The night was young.

Later, I managed to shuffle/body pop my way over to chat. I'm not a body popper. It got a smile out of him. Let me explain, my singirls. This was your typical gym giant. Over six feet of pure muscle, testosterone and ego. I had to have him. Thus, began my unsubtle flirting until he realised that he wasn't going to escape without buying me a drink and getting my number. The missing buttons helped focus his attention on my heart and the shortness of said dress on my arse. Call it vodka confidence but by the end of the night I knew he would call.

Now part of the reason I live alone is because I'm not a quiet person. Ask my neighbours. Music blasting, constant '80s pop-inspired dance breaks, loud cooking as I look for cooking thingies and general noises of one who enjoys life vocally. In my flat I can sing. And I sing like any diva – loudly.

When the giant finally visited, I was expecting big things. I heard all about the gym routine. He had a spare room full of gym equipment. I had a spare room full of fancy-dress outfits and was allergic to gyms. It was never going to be a love match but as I carefully explained to him as long as we were a horizontal match who cared about the rest of it. And so, our workout began.

I had to give him his dues. He was big where it mattered, had stamina for days and was strong enough to lift me. The workout was going surprisingly well. But then he just stopped and dismounted, inelegantly at that. Apparently, he was finished. I hadn't heard a peep or a grunt out of him. Maybe my sex iTunes mix was on too loud? As he went to clean up, I rushed to switch it off.

Pillow talk discarded and we were ready for round two. Take note my singirls, pillow talk with gym giants really isn't something you should let him lead on. I found out more about protein drinks than I ever needed to. Round two and again I'm seeing great form from him, a little more effort from me and a focus on longevity. I had high hopes. But then, was he... counting? I stopped my moans of appreciation and yes, there it was again. He was doing stroke repetitions! Thrust deep on 10. Hmm, I was about to raise it but then I didn't want him to lose his rise and so I went with it. I wasn't miserable. At least this time I wouldn't miss the crescendo and big finish. And then I saw it. The pained, constipated expression men get before release. This was it, so close and then... nothing. Not even a squeal. Another inelegant dismount (he really needs to work on that – 4.2 from the Chelsea Judge) and he swaggered off.

He was a silent lover. No talking, no big finish, no communication. This to him really was a workout but without the grunting and mirrors. That said I'm sure he wouldn't have minded mirrors. It unnerved me. I realised that I'm big on communication during sex. We don't need a running commentary but some sort of indication of progress, encouragement, appreciation is needed. Don't get me wrong, my singirls, he was a great fu** buddy for some months and I even managed to lose a few pounds, but there is a reason I don't love the gym. It's too clinical and controlled. I prefer a dance class where I can feel the music and sing along badly to '90s R & B. Oh, who am I kidding? You know me too well – '80s pop it is.

Hmmm, perhaps I should get more mirrors?

Watford Gap

I wasn't going to write about this one but then he spotted some of my posts on Facebook and insisted that I didn't write about him. So, I promptly ignored him.

I met him on one of those 'chatty chatty' sex sites where everyone calls you babe and tells you how horny they are. They all want to send you videos of them wanking and think that porn is staple TV viewing. Bored with the predictable, I was pleasantly surprised when he just said hi and chatted like a normal person as opposed to one who was in mid stroke/porn climax. Reading his profile, he seemed fine except the location. Watford! Urgh – outside my 45-minute travel rule.

However, he hadn't annoyed me in three hours, so I jumped onto National Rail to check out the travel times. Hmm, it sounds far but door to door I could do it on the train in 44 minutes. This included him picking me up at the airport – I mean, the train station which he said he was more than happy to do. He even had the decency to tell me in advance that he'd lied on his profile and wasn't 36.

He was 46. This was after I told him that the one thing I couldn't abide by was a man who lied. So, there was an age gap too. This wasn't looking good at all. It would be one dinner and I was flying back to London.

I wasn't expecting much at all, but he was lovely. He let me have the remote control whenever I visited and was always available for a last-minute hook up. He also warmed the sheets for me as I have developed severe separation anxiety from Lekky, my electric blanket. He constantly had snacks and hot water and it was really the ideal set up. So much so that one night I found myself calling my boyfriend Addison Lee and paying to get up there. That's when I realised that one of my reasons for not travelling more than 45 minutes was financial. I was clearly in the middle of a dating recession.

He shared his own dating woes and I realised that women weren't the only ones that had it tough. What's with women over-sharing on the gynaecological issues? Men don't care. It's either you are going to shag or you aren't. Don't gross out lovers with bodily details.

Things were going well with regular, no-pressure sex meetups. It helped that we supported the same football team when *Champions League* was on and were both divorced, so no silly divorce questions.

But then birthdays came and we had to tell each other what we wanted. I honestly can't remember what I wanted but he wanted to buy me a gigolo. Such a thoughtful gift but I wasn't going to let a lover choose another lover. Then he said what he would like… a threesome.

Yawn. I wasn't averse to the idea but here's the thing. They aren't that easy to organise? But he was such a sweetie that I went straight into 'girl-with-a-plan' mode. I found an ad for another girl who was looking for a threesome and I said that I would be willing to be the guest star for her show if she would reciprocate. It was a done deal. I told him all about it and he started to get excited but then after I guest starred in her fantasy, I realised that I wasn't keen on seeing her again and cancelled the reciprocal visit.

Watford Gap said he understood but let's face it, I hadn't delivered on my threesome birthday gift promise. A night in watching Justin Slayer with two Brazilian girls just isn't the same as being the star of the show yourself.

Like all good things it ended. Casual sex just wasn't going to cut it when the pressure was on for me to deliver grandbabies. Now every time I travel through Watford Junction, I think of him warming the sheets for me… and it warms my heart a little.

See, they aren't all bad, are they?

Valentine's Guy Two

There are times in the year that are just not for the single girl. Valentine's Day is one of those times. The constant questions from well-meaning loved ones and smugly paired off couples on whether or not you're seeing anyone are multiplied as that dreaded date looms nearer.

Remember I told you about my double Valentine's? Number One was lazy cheap and didn't last past the date, but what happened to sweet Valentine's Number Two of the card and knickers? Well he lived four hours away during the week. Perfect! This freed up my weeks for after-work dates, hanging with the girls, healthy doses of pampering myself and something else… oh yeah, work.

Valentine's Number Two sold himself as the last of the classic romantics. I told him that I was a cynical romantic but we had something in common: a healthy appreciation for his physical attributes. Don't judge me, singirls. Some men are just more blessed than others.

All was well until we decided to switch things up and go to his place. I walked into a house far up in North London only to find a Hugh Hefner wannabe nightmare. A white leather sofa with a zebra throw greeted me. The dining room was a full gym, the cupboards were full of Pro Max body building powders and he was forced to rush out and get an emergency stock of vodka and cranberry to cure my more than mild panic. Upstairs, the bedroom was all fitted *faux*-silk black sheets and mirrors everywhere! Perhaps this is what was fashionable… in 1979.

Just when I thought it couldn't get any worse, I discovered that he and his roommate wanted a threesome. There are many things I would do my precious but a girl with a plan needs *ages* to plan something of that magnitude. Besides, I had seen the home gym. These guys were strong health freaks. Then he got a call and rushed out. After surreptitiously checking his wardrobes for any bondage gear, I tried to shake off my suspicions that there was something amiss in this house.

Two shags later, I spotted he had fallen asleep and his phone was left on the side. Who had he been talking to for 20 minutes outside? I checked the last calls made and realised that the call from his boss on a Sunday was actually from a girl called Carol. Was she on her way over to turn the non-threesome into a foursome? Can anyone say entrapment?

So, I did what any self-respecting girl would do when he woke up and started hinting about the roommate. I turned one wrong word from him into a monumental argument and promptly went to sleep threatening his manhood if he touched me again. The next day I ran out of there and *never* looked back. Classic romantic? Classic prick more like.

The moral of the tale is if you must play away do so within taxi distance of home. And sometimes a little diva gets you out of a sticky situation like a threesome.

—❤—

14. Fools

This chapter could be so, so much longer as I came across a lot of fools on my adventures. Some were so blatantly foolish that I never bothered to reply to their emails. Sadly, there were many I did engage with but soon learned that they were either not that serious or were that dumb. I particularly came to hate all of those guys who blatantly disregarded everything I said I wanted and said things like "I'm Bjorg, 53 from Amsterdam. I love women with chocolate skin. I want to lick you all over," or, "I'm over 45, married with kids and Asian. How about it? Want to see a picture of my cock?" No, I really don't dude and neither does your wife by the sounds of things. But they weren't all internet dates as you will see below.

The Smell

Please be warned there are scenes of a distressing nature here. Well, I was distressed anyway.

There are clues to look for when you're internet dating. Old worn photos from another era, claims of a height under five foot nine (everyone knows men add two to four inches onto everything so they're likely five foot four) and then there are those that think they are Richard Blackwood. Dated humour with unoriginal observations.

But this, one my singirls, sounded perfect. Yes, he was a wee bit young and lived at home but I could forgive that. We are, after all, in the midst of a recession. Or so my accountant kept reassuring me. He also had a job and lived within the required 45-minute date zone in Clapham. He claimed to be from West Africa. I have since learned that this was code for Nigerian. But he was saying all the right things and it was a sexual date. He promised me a night filled with orgasms and I promised that I would think about it. I'd become cautious by this stage.

We agreed to meet in Battersea as that was where my once favourite first date haunt, Revolution Bar, was. It was near to the buses and station and had large enough windows that meant you could see your intended date approach and exit stage left if necessary.

I arrived first, though ten minutes fashionably late. I ordered my cranberry juice (never drink till you've met you're intended victim) and in walked… The Smell.

I called him The Smell because as he entered the doors of the bar something in the air changed. At first, I thought it was the electrical charge from his psychosis-induced afro, but one look and I knew that the evening was doomed. He walked up to me and I couldn't help but take a sniff of the air. Was that… his breath?!

He went in for the air kisses and I tried to duck but before I knew it, he'd kissed me near my mouth. The smell enveloped me and lingered. This was the 'dead-gutter-rat-in-the-intestine-type' halitosis. I thanked the dating gods that I had refused dinner and as he sat down, I wondered if I would ever eat again.

Turns out The Smell had other ideas. He quickly revealed that although he lived with his parents, he had a key to his younger sister's place and if all went well was hoping that we would end up there that night. I ran through feasible excuses. Despite my discomfort, I managed to stretch it out to about 25 minutes gulping down fresh air as I drank my cranberry juice. I was raised to be polite. He breathed and wordily retold the rancid tales of many a dating disappointment. He had lost his job three weeks prior. I tried to think quickly but the smell left my brain cells weakened. So, I pulled the lame work excuse.

He looked disappointed as we walked to the station. Struggling for composure, I tried to edge forwards as we waited on the platform for the train. Then I felt him press himself against my backside, letting out a sigh (breath) on my neck and this raised interest of his quickly lowered my staunch politeness. I screamed, "No!" like one of those women in self-defence classes and ran like Flo Jo onto the train. I didn't even say goodbye – I just jumped on board and was finally able to breathe.

There is breathless with lust, my singirls, and then there is fighting for air. Worse, he had ruined Revolution Bar for me.

The Flasher

I'm not easily scared or intimidated. Well that's not true. But by now I've seen so much sexually that I can hide my fear. That being said, I am a woman and some things still catch me completely off guard.

One day on my way back from a job in Woolwich, I was waiting on the train platform for the train back to London Bridge. As I stood in the same spot as

131

I did every day reading my latest novel of choice, I was oblivious to the man who came up next to me until he asked me if my book was nice. I gave him a distracted "Yes, thank you," and went back to finding out what embarrassing thing Poppy was about to do to get Harry to notice her now that she'd given him a makeover and realised that he was actually the one. Yes, this was the extent of my daily reading material. No Fanon for this chick. It turns out that Poppy was about to interrupt Harry with her best friend who had recognised that the new Harry was hot way before Poppy had. Why hadn't I seen that story line coming?

The train finally arrived, and I sat in a section by the window with the man sat opposite me. He was West African, in his 40s, slightly built and not unattractive, but I just wasn't interested. I dove back into my book when my cousin called me from South Africa. As we caught up, I noticed the man fiddling with his newspaper. That was one interesting *Evening Standard* I thought, as I chatted away.

Still oblivious to his intent, I laughed as my cousin regaled me with stories of at the latest family gossip. Distracted by the newspaper rustling again, I looked up and there his dick was, hanging out of his jeans looking at me like I should be impressed. He hid it from the other travellers with his newspaper. Who knew an *Evening Standard* would come in so handy? What the f*ck was wrong with this fool?! This was no way to start a conversation with a stranger.

I honestly didn't know what to do, so I explained to my cousin what was going on, and he was like, "Sis, move into another carriage." Woken from my paralysis, I moved into another part of the train and squashed myself between two people who looked like they would be good in a tussle. That was a long train journey home. Well it was minutes, but it felt a lot longer.

Eventually I got home and the full extent of what had happened hit me. But being pragmatic, I figured I hadn't been touched and it was over. Or so

I thought. Firstly, I ended up not sleeping well as flashbacks of the flasher were haunting me. I don't know what about it bothered me so much except that I hadn't been sexually intimidated like that before so publicly.

Then I saw him a few weeks later and realised that he was a local. It could easily happen again I thought and so I reported it to the Woolwich Po Po who are in no way worthy of the same shout out as the C&W Po Po. They sent me a letter about Victim Support and chided me for not reporting it sooner as apparently, they have cameras on the trains but change them every 14 days. Good to know. Their advice was to move away from the perpetrator, report it immediately and not to panic as most flashers aren't violent. Erm, yeah thanks for that.

And thus, ends another sad tale on unnecessary and unsolicited male attention and behavioural deficit.

The Virtual Dick

We met on one of those adult friend sites. I know my singirls, but he was hot. He told me he was well hung and sent text pictures to validate his claims. Oh, and he was British Born Naija. I really couldn't ask for more from a potential friend with benefits.

But then he insisted that I wasn't to fall in love. Apparently, every woman he met fell in love with him. The arrogance of the man. Didn't he realise that not all women are looking for love from every man we meet? No, we quickly decide if you are a friend, a fuck or the FuHu.

I assured him that I would fight any love-based urges and so we arranged to meet. On the day, I waited for the confirmation text/call/Facebook message but I didn't hear from him. Had I been virtually stood up? Later that night, he sent me a message saying that his friend had cancer and he'd been in the hospital with her all day as she was dying.

Now, I'm no medical expert but something about this didn't ring true. What he didn't know was that I talked to a lot of people, so when he told me more about his friend, I corroborated his story with doctors and pharmacists who told me that the worst thing his friend had was the flu or food poisoning. I deleted him immediately cursing myself for falling for a smile and a big dick... again.

But then a year later and I had forgotten how ridiculously he had lied. Debating as to whether or not I should believe him, when the friend request came in, I saw that smile and caved. I mean really, who would f*ck with karma so much and make up The Big C to get out of a date? Maybe he'd been confused. And so, my singirls, I began the dance of the penis text messages and late-night flirtations.

We agreed to meet again and I figured that surely, even he wouldn't be rude enough to cancel on me twice. We were practically friends. Well, we had 245 mutual friends! But alas, this guy was surrounded by ill health as he again missed our date without explanation and later told me that... his dog was ill, and he had to rush her to the vet. I suspect that like his friend with cancer, his dog had a mysterious 24-hour ailment that would clear up the next day.

Now again I'm no veterinary expert but I've studied men and realised that whilst he loved flirting online, he clearly wasn't going to come out from behind the safety of his phone. Either that or his girlfriend/partner/wife wouldn't let him out to play. What ever happened to saying you had to work late?

But never trust a man who doesn't believe in the power of karma my singirls. Or a guy who sends you photos of his dick. No matter how big.

The Nollywood Date

I can't say that I have much time for Nollywood since my encounter with an obsessed fan. After weeks of internet flirting, we met at a bar and there was an awful lot more flesh than I was used to; Maxine Su was feeling decidedly anorexic in comparison. He told me that the photos he'd sent were not of his torso but those of a cousin. What's with the false pretence?

Anyway, we danced, drank and agreed to meet again. I wasn't going to but he'd admitted that his recent weight gain was because work had been hectic, so he hadn't been to the gym. I thought about my own annual trip to the gym and ignored the fact that he kept bumping me with his belly every time he laughed. He invited me around for dinner and I don't miss an opportunity to get a home-cooked meal that hasn't been burned by me. Maybe it was the cocktails but I was feeling more gracious than usual and acquiesced.

So, after three hours prep, I turned up at his Hendon place (first mistake) on a Friday night looking effortlessly post work. No need for him to know I'd sat in my PJs all day. He buzzed me in, and he was...in his PJs? Really? And not the good sort of PJs either. No. These were the stained ex-gym gear mix-and-don't-match variety PJs. I didn't smell anything cooking and the lounge said that he and his Xbox were settled in for the night.

I sat down and asked him what was for dinner. He said pizza. I told him that I was lactose intolerant. He said "Oh!" and was back to the Xbox. At least, I think it was an Xbox. I quickly got bored and decided to explore his DVD collection. Surprisingly, I didn't recognise one title and that was because they were all Nollywood films. To distract him from *Hounds of Fisty Screams* or whatever game he was playing, I asked him about his DVDs, and it worked! He switched off the contraption, bunged in the pizza (not one of Tesco's Finest) and started showing me his favourite Nollywood clips, laughing incessantly and telling me about his Nollywood babes' sexual fantasies... in great detail too.

Spurred on by his fantasies he decided it was time for the pin and lunge game which meant that his lips and stomach pinned me to the sofa. All I remember was his full stomach pressing into my now hungry concave tummy. I struggled and he pushed me further still into the 20-year-old sofa. Oh, if that sofa could talk, I'm sure it would have thanked me for giving it a break from his fat arse sitting on it listlessly for hours playing games.

Though I realised that despite there being zero chemistry, he still thought I was up for a fumble. I wasn't. I finally managed to release a hand, tear his lips away from mine and ask about the pizza. As he went to investigate, I grabbed my phone and made up an excuse to leave. I think my non-existent cat had its seventh illness that night. I called my Addison Lee and as I turned to say goodbye, I realised that he had already forgotten me. It was now him, his pizza and the babes of Nollywood. I don't think Nollywood men are for me, my singirls. I prefer to be the star of any date.

P.S. I heard from Nollywood a few days later and like so many of them he wasn't aware that things hadn't gone that well. I need to work on my communication because either I'm not clear or they are just blatant chancers who figure because it's casual they can be more disrespectful than normal and get away with it. That was not how this was going to work for me.

The Cuban

So, it was a big date night and I wanted to make sure that everything went to plan. I was ready to meet a guy whose Spanglish texting and over-excited pleas to be my lover were quite endearing.

Cute underwear? Check.
An outfit that says you know you want to and just on the wrong side of tight? Check, check.

136

Useful Spanish phrases:

Don't stop – *no pares*

Right there – *mas duro*

It's so big – *Que grande la tienes* (tick only if it applies)

Check, check, check.

I arrived in Kentish town at 8.30 at night and after spending some money on vodka cranberry, he took me to a nice flat… which he shared with his religious auntie. He told me we had to be quiet but luckily, she wasn't in, 'cos I told him that if it went well, I couldn't help but make noise. I ignored the stale smell of weed and the bikini clad posters. Do men stull have those posters?

So, we started off with him teaching me to salsa. Within minutes, this had digressed into heavy petting and both of us naked. It was on! He was very attentive and all about the foreplay. *Bingo*! Then, just as I was primed the tricky condom moment came up. His strategy was just to go forth and conquer whereas I, like all good women do not go out without a raincoat. It's an afro hair thing. Turns out he didn't have any and never used them. I reluctantly climbed off his hot, fit sticky frame and started putting my clothes back on over the pink lace Gossard number I used to impress.

Then, just when I thought it couldn't get any worse, his religious aunt came back and had brought her church with her. Twenty minutes later, there was no escaping it. I had to say hi and leave with everyone thinking they knew what went on in that room. In turn, I wanted to shout back that we actually didn't have sex 'cos my parents raised me right, unlike the wastrel nephew.

At 10pm, I was almost back at my house when I had a brainwave. Why waste all that good foreplay? I called up an old f*** buddy just to see how he was doing. But as he eagerly picked up the bait, I realised that I was underprepared for a spontaneous booty call. I would have to make the bed, do the dishes and change my lingerie. He'd already seen the pink Gossard set.

The most worrying thing about The Cuban was that he wouldn't tell me his age and insisted that age didn't define him. This made him about 45. The other worrying thing was that he told me as we walked back to the station that he never ever used condoms, as he could tell which girls were healthy and didn't have STDs and those that weren't healthy and had STDs. I was too frustrated at this point to tune into his theory because I realised that he was a LEE who got women horny then hoped that they would be polite enough to go through with it. I wasn't about to take that risk and we never ever spoke again.

So, I was home by 11 lamenting what almost was. Next time, I'll tidy my place and take my own condoms.

15. Films: My Life in Porn

Act 1: The Opening Scene

My first memory of porn was when I was nine or ten playing football on a field near our house. There were some woods and something special had been found there. Was it the pot of gold at the end of the rainbow? Was it a mysterious well of never-ending Twix? I rushed to see because even back then, there was nothing I liked better than being in on the next big thing. But no, it was a half-torn porn magazine which the boys pored over for ages. I wasn't sure why this was so special until one of the boys showed me a blonde woman standing staring at the camera with this come-hither look, topless. It was the eyes and the cute pink bikini bottoms that did it but, for a second, I felt a stirring of an understanding of her power over these pathetic boys. Women can be powerful. But that second passed, and I wanted to get back into the game. We (I was on the shirts team obviously) were winning and there was no sign of a Twix to keep me occupied. I quickly realised that porn was something that young boys immediately gravitated towards and could distract them from much more important things like winning in life. However, what with the tabloids and their page 3, I really wasn't sure why I was meant to be excited about a bit of flange.

I was a child before the watershed, so I remember that there was soft porn on TV when I was about seven but that hadn't even seemed like porn to me. It was two teenagers making love on some show that I saw whilst we were on our school holiday. Our nanny was hooked though and I discovered that women liked the romantic story stuff (would Paul and Michelle stay together? I never found out as my brother's giggling got us banished to the playroom). Men, on the other hand, just seemed to like to look.

Or so I thought.

Act 2: The Plot Thickens

Then, as I grew up in the VHS era it wasn't until university that I was exposed to it again. As you know my singirls, I led a very sheltered life. It did exist I'm sure but young boys would never deem it necessary to share porn with a mere girl they were dating. My teens were a porn-free zone. I was more into pop music and going out and showing off my well-rehearsed butterfly dance.

But at university a French-African guy invited me over to watch videos. We weren't friends just mild acquaintances and I didn't get any indication that he saw me as anything more than that slightly kooky kid. He was a mature student. As I went over, I was hoping for the new Sandra Bullock movie but instead was greeted by bad porn. This was before obsessive hair removal and there was still some dodgy retro music tracks. In those days you were lucky to get anything that wasn't American, Scandinavian or German. That's a point, what's happened to the Scandinavian porn industry? I digress.

We sat on the couch and I think I was supposed to be turned on as he edged closer, breathed heavily and pressed into my thigh. Instead I was in tears of hysterics. This was the best comedy ever! There was no way this beautiful if somewhat trailer park woman wanted to have sex with that old dude with the pale hairy skin and the fat but short knob. Where was his butt? Urgh! And yet she tried to sound convincing, bless her. I was a university student and did what I did best – gave a critical analysis. I dissected their acting, the plot which was vague and not particularly believable and the décor This is why to this day I can't do Eastern European and Russian porn. Why? The décor is so post-communist non-chic it puts me off. I just want to go in there and do one of those 60-minute makeovers. And don't even get me started on their wigs. Anyway, eventually my host stopped with the heavy breathing and offered to take me home. I giggled and asked if there was any more popcorn. Maybe I just needed something more realistic? It was all a bit far-fetched for me, and on top of that, none of the actresses looked like me. They were all blonde and size zero. I just wanted to feed them. So clearly, I still hadn't gotten the point of porn.

Act 3: The Voyeur

Living with a partner makes getting some alone time rather difficult. It's funny because whenever I wanted to get off without him, I would tell him that I needed some me time and go upstairs. But this was too mature for him. When he wanted his me time, he would sneak off upstairs a few times and I assumed it was for a cheeky cigarette or to buy me a surprise gift online but no, it was to watch porn. One day I burst in on him after my shopping trip was cut short by one of my cards not working. And there he was on a site that I didn't recognise. His preference worryingly was for younger girls. I should have seen it as a sign as his girlfriends are now getting younger as he gets older. Porn files are key my singirls. But no, he wasn't willing to share. Instead he enjoyed sneaking around and having a wank to women with no breasts and lanky blonde hair. Not my thing so I left him to it and instead monopolised the big screen TV to catch up

141

on world affairs such as *Spendaholics* and the *Biggest Loser US*. Getting off on watching others comes in many forms. I preferred to watch people being told off by experts and berated for the sad state of their lives. Don't judge. To me this was much better than porn.

Act 4: Shake That Ass, Girl

One day I was staying over at an ex's and he said I could work from his computer. I can't remember what site I was trying to get onto, but I keyed in the first few letters and a whole heap of sites came up which started with black: blackbooty, blackbabewithbutts, etc. Intrigued I quickly forgot about my work deadline and instead explored his internet history. I was greeted by a sea of, well, black booties. What else would there be? Suddenly all of our sex till then made so much sense. He was living out the fantasy of his porn. I on the other hand had spent way too much time with my head in a pillow wondering what he was doing back there. The porn talk only came later.

Eventually he agreed to show me his favourite downloaded clips (I learned to always check the desktop; apparently, they have to be accessible) and again I laughed as one of the scenes had a group of the director's friends eating chicken in the background, as a stepdad seduced his wayward stepdaughter. It was a little too reality porn for my tastes. Where was the fantasy porn that made you think that everyone had mansions, clear heels and a wardrobe full of fancy dress? That's what I wanted to see. And hadn't these people heard of body paint or foundation? I know razor bumps, dirty heels and stretch marks are keeping it real but it was all just not that much of a turn on.

Act 5: The Porn Star

So then, years later I was greeted with the results of men watching too much porn *aka* The Wannabe Porn Star. What was wrong with these men who thought watching it was enough to make him as good as Lexington Steele or Mr Marcus? I wish he acted like a porn star because that might have made it all the more convincing but no, instead, he chose to only speak like a porn star. I wanted to tell him that he needed to shag like one too but male... ego... fragile.

The problem with men who talk like porn stars is that unlike in the movies where the women have their own lines like, "Yes Big Daddy, I want you to f*ck me up the ass so much! I want you to f*ck me and then come on my face" [*voice breathless and schoolgirl-esque*], they don't really inspire the average woman into getting into character. If you're merely a mediocre lover then chances are this won't work. So, as he fed me lines about how much I deserved his cock 'cos I had worked hard for it, my mind was reeling thinking, *Did I miss an email from him with my lines?* Oh, and just to keep it authentic he kept his white sports socks on as all good black porn stars do. I didn't keep my heels on as I was more worried about my sheets. I just can't be flung into a movie set without some sort of preparation, my singirls.

Act 6: The Money Shot

And so, I left him and decided to go on my own porn exploration. The problem with a lot of porn is that it's for men. Women in porn may be billed as the stars but they are just a vessel for men to live out their fantasies. I tried the made for female porn and that was horrendous. How much soft lighting and elevator music do they think women want? It was all becoming a bit too *Mills and Boon* for me with the tender lovemaking as if it was an instructional educational video. Don't get me wrong, I know we love a story but most of these people can't act and I don't need that much justification as to why she would sleep with a vampire.

And then it hit me. I'm all about the story, the seduction, the outfits, not the actual sex itself. I watch it like I do any other movie (i.e., to be entertained). Yes, I can get off on it on a voyeuristic level and sometimes we all just need to take the edge off a hard day, but I am a woman. I watch porn the way I have sex: with meaning. It's not about the one where they are just fucking and I'm meant to think, *Yeah that could be me being fucked by that guy who doesn't give a shit about her and is just doing her so that guys everywhere can get off.* The guys aren't generally as hot as the women are, so aesthetically it's a fail there. What's in porn for women? Not enough I say.

And yet I persist in my search for the ultimate porn clips. Note clips 'cos I don't have time for 90 minutes of mediocre-to-bad acting where clothes fall off in the street or they decide to make someone a werewolf for no reason at all.

Porn is great for exploring what turns you and your partner on, but could I see myself living a life without it? Yes, because at the end of the day the real thing, whether it's sex or making love is always much more fun. I guess I'm not much of a voyeur then.

Happy Watching!

P.S. I'm going through a Melissa Monet phase. One clip of her doing her daughter's boyfriend was brilliant once you got past her annoying acting. In fact, I may just go watch that now… be back in 38 minutes.

16. Forward Looking

Sex for the sake of sex was nice for a wee while but I realised that I wasn't the sort of person to sustain it for long. I actually like hanging out, watching DVDs with one person and cooking crap they have to eat because they love me. The other thing I liked more was going out, which was much more fun with the girls. And so, I started reflecting on my dating research.

The Cock Call

Last night I was booty-called. Yes, I know my singirls, I'm appalled too. Not because it shouldn't happen but because this was a guy I hadn't heard from in three weeks, who I'd had bad sex with ages ago and who now thought it was OK to call me at 2.30am asking if I want company. No!

I told him I couldn't because I'd given up sex for Lent. I doubt he believed me. Anyway, it got me to thinking about booty calls and why there's a thin line between an acceptable one and an insulting one. I think the key for me is that there needs to be a build-up. Send a text earlier in the day perhaps or a bit of Twitter banter to grease the wheels. But a booty call out of the blue is not the one.

Then I got to thinking about me and my cock-calling exploits of times past. If a woman calls you after a certain time of night know that it's not a booty call. We don't want the booty. We want the cock. I know you're never sure if this is just a precursor to us wanting more and robbing you of your independence but trust me, sometimes we just want the cock. But be warned, not all women do. You're right to be cautious.

So here you go guys. There are some checks to make to understand that cock call that may be coming to a phone near you.

If you get a call and it sounds like this:

Him: Hello?

Her: Hey, I was just thinking about you. What you doin'?

Him: Nothing, just chilling playing on some stupid games console that I'm way too old for. You?

Her: Nothing much. Ah, so you fancy coming 'round?

... At that point, know she's horny and make a plan to go over. But first, Check One:

1. How drunk is she?

If the call is more like this:

Him: Hello?

Her: Singing, "How did you know, cos I never told, you found out I got a crush on you," or,

Her: Hey gorgeous. You're so sexy. Why don't you bring that hot body of yours 'round so that I can bleep, then I'll grab that sexy arse of yours and bleep, bleep, bleep, bleep.

Then chances are she is on the right side of drunk and it is safe to proceed. This is the sort of drunk when she'll be freakishly dirty but not emotional. It's a win-win. She'll be slightly shy in the morning but you'll have had a good night so what do you care.

If, however the call goes something like this:

Him: Hello?

Her (sobbing): XX you know I love you! Why can't you just love me as much as I love you (pig like sob)? We would be *soo* good together and not just when we're making love and you do that thing where you get me to suck your balls whilst you watch porn and, in the daytime too (more pig snort sobs). I've spoken to my mum/therapist/bitter single best friend and she says I need to tell you exactly how I feel. Can you come 'round so we can talk about it?

Here I suggest you fake a dodgy connection, switch off your phone and go back to punching strangers and attacking them with balls of fire. Now for Check Two.

2. The fuel situation

I'm not talking about your petrol although that's not an unreasonable assumption to make. But listen, as I'm someone who survives on snacks and thinks three glasses of champagne and some Haribos constitutes a full meal, mine is not the place to come without bringing your own supplies. The only thing I have mastered to the standard that I'm willing to share is the big English breakfast. So, if the sex is amazing you may get rewarded.

You guys however require constant sustenance to keep yourself going throughout the night. At least that's the excuse we women keep hearing for some lacklustre performances. I guess it's because you lose a teaspoon of protein and sweat all over our sheets, therefore food is a necessity. My advice? Stop off and bring a takeaway. It's the least you can do to again avoid the emotion trap and much better than flowers or a bottle of booze. You know your performance decreases by 20% on booze.

If you're asking her to cook for you, be warned that you are entering into the realms of a relationship. If you are going to restaurants before or after a cock/booty call, also dangerous. Inevitably the need to discuss the sex will come up and that never ends well for the man. Trust me. You say you wouldn't mind trying anal, she says she wouldn't mind trying a relationship and it's all over. Keep talking to a minimum. Just do that thing you do so well, where you roll over and play dead whilst snoring and hogging the blanket. Nothing says just sex more than that. Finally, Check Three.

3. Condomise

Now I know I preach about this all the time but why do you leave your house to go somewhere else, pass many a Tesco Express and a 24-hour pharmacy, manage to stop off at KFC and yet still reach a woman's house without condoms? This is not a good look. If you come over looking like you could potentially have sex without a condom then again you are venturing into a conversation about what this all means.

If she's clever she will have hidden her real desire for a relationship or even better may not deem your cock worthy of its own face cloth but, do you really want to take the risk here guys? Sex without a condom is tantamount to a declaration of love, trust and affection. Make sure we know that it's sex and nothing but sex. So, bring your own condoms and stop being so cheap.

That's it. The three checks for a successful cock call. I'm going back to bed to catch up on my interrupted sleep. Oh, and if she is calling you after 3am, forget it. By the time you get there she'll be fast asleep. Trust me.

The Sex Test

So today I got a fright; my singirls, for an hour of my life I lost my fabulousness.

It started well. Waking up singing 'Hakuna Matata', I remembered that I'd had a heap of blood tests done and was yet to get the results. So I called and they said I needed to come in and collect my requested letter. I like to show prospective partners that I take my sexual health seriously and so should they.

My trouble with the NHS isn't the professionals. It's the receptionists. I arrived and she looked at her computer screen and told me that my tests appeared normal but that I needed to see the doctor. What for? She wasn't sure. I asked for a printout and started to worry when I saw her going off to find the ink cartridge and rig up an industrial antique looking printer. This was going to take a while but I wasn't worried. I'd always been careful.

The printout I got was nothing short of a confused mess. I asked her what it all meant, and she looked at me pityingly and said I needed to see the doctor.

There were negatives and positives everywhere and by the looks of things I had hepatitis B and syphilis! She could give me an appointment next week. Well my singirls, I'm not one for diva outbursts but... I demanded to see someone and within an hour was back fuming but ready to face the news.

That was the worst hour of my life. I thought back and since my last tests, I'd only been with two partners both of whom I'd been safe with. But then... you never know. I planned my phone calls to both cursing them out but telling them they needed to get to a clinic *asap*. I looked up treatments and didn't fancy penicillin shots into my buttocks but gulping, I figured that's the least I deserved. Hep B was going to be a whole lot harder to get rid of. Oh, that was a long hour and thanks to search engines, very informative. I know Dr Google isn't the best source of information but when you're faced with receptionists like this one, what is one to do?

It turns out that all my tests were clear, and I didn't have anything at all. The industrial antique printer had jumped a line and I had antibodies against rubella and chicken pox. I've never been so happy to have had the chicken pox even though at the time none of the kids would play with me at Pontins.

But I've learned my lesson my singirls. I called some exes and told them of my decision to abstain from sex for a while. This met with ridicule, disbelief and protests that I couldn't deny them like that, but I've realised that no cock is worthy of having to go through that hour.

So, stay safe my singirls and beware the antique printers and receptionists at doctor's surgeries.

If I Were a Boy

I've always thought what sort of man I would be if I were a man but knowing the things I know as a woman. What would work and what wouldn't? Let's face it most men don't think women are that bright when it comes to interactions so I guess I would assume the same? Not that I want to be a man as the thought of having to feign enthusiasm about computer games, films in space/hobbit land or shave my face every day doesn't really sell it. But if I woke up and had a penis (mine would be of a size) then I think I would be an undercover playa. Yes, indeed I would be the ultimate dog and my singirls this is how I would do it.

1. I would have loads of women that I was talking to at the same time. Rotation baby, rotation. Otherwise women can get boring 'cos they want to talk all the bloody time about things I don't care about. Plus, options mean none of them become a priority even though bless 'em they would think they are the one. Wait, would I still say bless 'em? Hmm...

2. I would call all women *my lovely, babes, sweetie* or *gorgeous* to avoid tripping up. But I would put them under my phone as a guy's names to avoid those that check for other women. I know that trick.

3. I would have two phones: one for the serious people in my life and the other for the floozies. I would tell floozies that the other was a work phone and therefore not to be used ever! Ever bitch! I'd snarl so she knew I was serious.

4. I would tell them all straight that I'm still in pain from another relationship and that I don't know if I can love again (cue Bambi eyes and sob story of betrayal from the only woman I've ever loved). I would then accept the consolatory sex they offered but not stay over. It's too soon.

5. I would market myself cheaply on Facebook and Twitter with some old photos from when I used to go to the gym. Shirtless works best. I would

post philosophical bullshit like 'you don't know what you've got till it's gone' or 'a real man doesn't lie or cheat' and let them come to me.

6. I would shower a lot to avoid detection. Some women and their strong perfumes!

7. I would buy them all the same perfume for birthdays and Christmas and tell them all to wear it to avoid detection.

8. I would tell her about all my friends that she will never ever meet but that I'm always with 'cos you know at 43 I still need to go to football training four times a week like there is an FA Cup to play for.

9. If I felt that she was getting suspicious, I would send her flowers or find an obscure poem online about eyes and send that to her. Fuck it, the poem is better, like I don't have enough bills going out of the house.

10. I would let her come first the first time to give the impression that I give a fuck. After that it's all about me baby!

11. I would do chivalrous things like open doors and pay for things. Then I know she's going to think I'm a gentleman and drop the panties sooner.

12. I would have two properties, one for my real life and the other for my bitches and one-night stands. Alternatively, I would just tell her I live at home so she couldn't stay over. I spend most of my time at mum's anyway.

13. I would only shag women who had their own places and preferably with kids. They seem more grateful for the opportunity and less likely to try to lock you down on the marriage tip for fear you'll disappear like the last guy.

14. I would train her by never calling more than once a week and only texting back two or three days later. Otherwise they get too attached and start thinking you and she are dating or something. What's that about?

15. I would have three or four basement restaurants where no one would ever be likely to see us and take them all there. Tell her it's my favourite spot.

16. If I was married, I would claim that we were going through a divorce or separated. This would gain me loads of sympathy. I would have to be careful not to appear too bitter though 'cos then they start thinking that they don't have a chance. Always leave them thinking there is a small chance. Women love the emotionally wounded.

17. I would drive. That way I can always be stuck in traffic (getting a last-minute blow job) or broken down (this shit is so good I'm going to have to stay for another round).

18. I would declare my love when drunk so that I could take it back when sober. Or better yet, never make mention of it 'cos I don't need to have that conversation.

19. I would always make sure I wore condoms 'cos these women are always trying to tie a brother down. But condoms are expensive so instead I would use the old 100% effective (not) withdrawal method and come on her face. But because I'm a playa I would avoid the hair. I don't need that kind of natural hair drama.

20. And finally, I would lie incessantly... because I can. Women give me permission to all the time. They always believe what they want to and if she goes, well then there is always Twitter or Facebook for me to find another. I don't even need to subscribe to those online dating sites anymore.

Peace out dudes (swaggers off with my big dick swinging 'cos if I were a boy, I would act like it was big even if it wasn't).

17. My Hubby

American Dream – How I Met Him

It was summertime and I was bored. I was in between jobs and naturally started to spend a lot more time on Facebook. There was a group that I'd been a member of for years which had suddenly been invaded by Black Americans. I know my singirls, I wasn't happy about it either. I tried to reengage but soon left as there were too many trolls and idiots for my patience to endure. Besides, it wasn't really for me. I just don't have that many ignorant statements to make about the rest of the world to compete. When you start talking about Africans and what they can learn from Western propaganda I zone out. It had quickly become one of those black means African-American groups.

Before I left the group, I made a few new friends and didn't really think much of it. Not long afterwards one started liking my posts more frequently and I, naturally, started stalking his page. He seemed normal. He had friends and family. This is all you can hope for in this day and age. A few months later, we started private messaging and before you knew it, boom! We were officially dating.

Now, as you know I have a 45-minute dating zone so dating someone who lived in the US and not even New York was a stretch at best. I wasn't really sure if it could work beyond Facebook but I made the classic error of phoning, visiting and doing everything first. These should have been warning signs. I've seen enough of Catfish to know that red flags aren't there because they look pretty. There was no video chatting before I got on the plane (he didn't have a computer with a webcam). I know. It was a huge risk.

Soon after Christmas, I booked a six-day Valentine's trip to the mid-west. I wasn't getting any younger and I didn't feel like I had time to waste. There was some hesitation on his part as he told me that he didn't have a bed. It had been a year since he had broken up with his girlfriend and he just had a mattress on the floor. He reassured me that he had all other furniture though and lived alone so I'd be OK.

My view was that I might as well see if this was worth it and, based on my first visit, it would seem so. Yes, he was nearly 40 minutes late to meet me at the airport and yes, we didn't really go out much but what new couple does? And there were some signs that money wasn't exactly flowing but, I argued, we are all coming off the back of a double-dip recession, right? I can't judge people on their economic status. Besides we got on and he loved '80s British music and *RuPaul's Drag Race* as much as I did so we had plenty to talk about.

I returned to the UK floating in love. It was time to prepare for the second visit and I did so promptly. He was yet to announce that he would visit me but that didn't faze me. I was a girl with a plan and a man who claimed he loved me. What more could I ask for? He also had a job which was time and place specific whereas mine was more flexible.

Let's be clear that there were a lot of things right about this person at the beginning. He said all the things you'd want to hear from a FuHu including that he was ready to hang up his player's badge and commit. I didn't doubt that the feelings were real. But as we all know men will say anything, they think you want to hear at the beginning of a relationship. Just like I'll actually make the effort of going to a salon at the beginning too. These visits drop off six months into most relationships. Yes, I'm a fraud.

But then I soon remembered that long-distance relationships take a lot more work than normal relationships. I'd forgotten as it had been a while since my last one. You have to be able to make sure that the person never feels bereft because you're not in their physical space. This is not hard to do these days with Skype and the joys of the android. But apparently it was too difficult for him to navigate sensibly and moving to the US was something that according to the US border control everybody wants to do. So, things started to get a little messy...

American Dream – Reality Bites

I really thought it would be different this time. We'd even set a wedding date (Well, I suggested a date when all of my family could make it and he agreed).

Despite my reservations about the land of the brave and free, I'd agreed to move to the land of reality TV, cronuts and plus-sized people. He'd agreed to meet Mama and Baba Black. Nothing says serious like agreeing to meet Baba Black! He told me that he'd booked a ticket to come and see me. Nothing says commitment to me than to leave a windy America for a wet London, right?

According to him, I was the one. The one he'd been waiting on, the one he'd asked the universe for. The mother of his yet to be conceived kids despite the constant trying. I believed him because I have a heart and he played to mine

157

perfectly. Telling me exactly what I needed to hear after years of wastemen. I'm a romantic. It really doesn't take much for me to believe you.

There were signs that not all was well. I suspected he had a drug habit far more serious than the odd puff of weed. The erratic behaviour with phone calls and money in general didn't help. But everyone knows that it takes a while to adjust to being in a relationship. He was cautious as his last relationship had lasted nearly a decade. After a breakup, he convinced me to take him back. Against my better judgement, I agreed. It didn't feel right but you can't expect everything to work smoothly straight away, right?

Then my birthday came along, and he promised to be the first person to call me. I waited. And waited. He wasn't. Apparently after months he couldn't work out the time difference and fell asleep. I asked myself, what drugs make people fall asleep?

Let's go back my singirls. Birthdays are so important to me that I have two. *Two*! I throw a party every year and I do a ten-day birthday countdown. There's even a song that I've been singing since university. I'm nothing if not precious about my birthday. But despite this being his chance to make it up to me, he just apologised and kept fucking up. Finally, I ignored the apologies. 'Nobody puts Baby Black in the corner' became my daily mantra.

I took to my status updates and spewed my dissatisfaction. Apparently, the snarky attitude he'd been drawn to some eight months before was now too bitchy and he needed to put me in check. So, he wrote me a really long email about his feelings and how he was putting me in check. I wrote back telling him he needed to get a life and stop living like a frat boy because for a man his age his behaviour wasn't acceptable. And how come he still didn't have a bed?

At this point, he declared that he would cancel his trip to the UK. Too much had been said for us to continue apparently. Wait, what? What kind of fight is over after two emails? Dude thought that was a breakup fight. I was just getting warmed up. But that was it. He was done and the way he went from being in love to being over it bewildered me. It was all about him and his feelings and he didn't give a shit about anyone else, least of all *moi*. Who was this dude and why didn't I recognise him as the same dude from a week before? The switch was creepy.

He claimed that he was going to get a refund on his plane ticket. That's when I knew he was a bare-faced liar. This was someone with an expired passport and no clue because, guess what, budget trips don't refund. Believe you me, I'd tried. By this point I figured that the plane money had been smoked away and this whole checking me was a way of starting an argument so that he could bounce. Yes, I picked up a few colloquialisms along the way much to Mama Black's chagrin. But he was set. It was over. He wasn't coming to visit me and he was sorry that he'd hurt me but, tough. I needed to understand his position.

Yeah fuck it, I was still mad. How dare this dude be all about marrying me, meeting the family, giving me kids and then two months later he's moved on? And did I mention that he'd borrowed nearly a grand? To keep his electricity on and pay his rent? I told you there were signs. His 'job' was a few hours of teaching at a college which barely paid the bills. He'd been working on the same creative project for 10 years to no avail and he was basically just a wasteman with better game and lyrics. (It took four months for him to pay me back all of my money and it only appeared after he got himself a new girlfriend so I'm guessing it was from her).

So, I spent a week sulking and wondering what I'd done wrong. Was it me? Maybe I should have not been such a snarky cow. But no, he got the edited version. The first three emails were declared 'unsendable' by my dating committee. So much of it didn't make sense. Was he just a crackhead whose love of drugs made him chaotic and randomly fall asleep? Were the night sweats (again – the red flags) really him in detox? Hell, I nearly took this idiot on a trip to Mexico with my friends for his birthday gift. My hard-earned money and I might have ended up arrested whilst he looked for a hit. Nah, that's not my life. But, despite it all I still felt hurt.

And then I realised that he was a narcissist! The kind of guy that builds you up buttercup just to let you down and mess you around. Hell, there's even a song that lays it out perfectly. Dating a narcissist means none of the shit he said about us and the future were ever true. He just wanted to lull me into a false sense of being in love and vulnerable. He thought he was smarter than me and for a while he was because I was stupid enough to think that no man lies about marriage. And it almost worked! But thanks to a bunch of friends who've let me cry on their virtual shoulders and a healthy amount of bad foods, I got better. I realised that there was nothing I had done that made this man the manipulative wasteman that he turned out to be. It made sense why his ex wouldn't speak to him anymore; she had a right to be angry as probably a lot of his stories had been bullshit. He was just a pathetic 40-something with a victim complex who realised that he wasn't going to get one over me and so disappeared at the first opportunity.

And so, with that knowledge, I was free from any of the guilt or wondering that comes with a sudden breakup. I realised that this is what some men do and was lucky to have escaped without having kids with a narcissist. Imagine having to explain his behaviour to a three-year-old?

I went away to Mexico anyway with family for a healing two weeks in the sun. A holiday we were meant to go on together. I let go of the relationship and was determined to come back to London ready for the next adventure.

American Dreams – Signs That You're Dating a Crackhead

Just to be clear, I don't have enough knowledge of drugs to know the difference between crack/crystal meth/speed, etc. What I do know from experience is that addicts, from alcohol to gambling and now drugs are sneaky, selfish and likely to make you think that you're crazy. But I have started to see that despite their best intentions, addicts can't hide their real love forever. Here are ways you too can spot the subtle and not so subtle signs.

When they talk about their drug wistfully... you're dating an addict

There are a number of conversations where drugs are discussed as an activity just before you start dating or during dating; however, this is only recreationally when his old friend tracks him down and forces them down his throat. Know that this isn't the first and won't be the last.

I didn't understand this story when I was told that an ex-con friend had bumped into him, then come over and persuaded him to have the drugs. But at the same time, he's telling you that he no longer does drugs, this ex-con knows where he lives and is coming over to smoke during the day?

When the landlord is knocking on the door... you're dating a crackhead

The beauty of the old-fashioned answering machine is that you too can hear the messages. Whilst I was over there, the landlord kept calling. The rent hadn't been paid. He ignored all the calls and said that whilst the rent was admittedly late, he wasn't more than a month over. Huh? This was turning into the beginnings of an episode of *The People's Court* and I'd found myself on the wrong side of the argument. Then, one day we were sitting there watching *Living Single* reruns and the landlord was knocking on the door. This confirmed that a), he was more than a month late, and b), the fact that he didn't even flinch meant that this had happened before.

When the other crackheads are knocking on the door... you're dating a crackhead

One day, late at night, whilst trying to figure out if I indeed had whatever ailment the long advert on TV was telling me I had, there was a knock on the door. Not the pesky landlord I hoped. No, this was a guy looking for a light. A light. At 10 at night. There was an exchange which I couldn't hear but needless to say, with hindsight, I reckoned that the dude wasn't just looking for a light. I was then told that this hadn't really happened before. I kept quiet and went back to wondering if I indeed had high blood pressure or terminal piles. Why were American medical adverts so bloody dramatic though?

When you spot the drug paraphernalia... you're dating a crackhead

So, on my first visit there was nothing to suggest that this person smoked cigarettes, let alone inhaled anything illegal. Then one day I was doing my usual inspection to ensure that there are no signs of another woman. I spotted an ashtray with a metal cigarette shaped thing in it and some dark powder. This didn't look like weed but university was a long time ago and besides, I was always too posh to actually buy my own drugs. I asked him and he told me something about it being a cigarette. This was perplexing to me as being an ex-smoker I knew what a cigarette and its ash looked like. It was also *not* the vapour one I'd bought him to help him quit which hadn't been spotted since I got here. Within seconds the ashtray disappeared, and I never saw it or metal cigarette again. In fact, I never ever saw him smoke. He just came back smelling of something I could never identify.

When he owes you money with little way of paying it back... you're dating an addict

After the breakup I became houndish about getting my money back. This may have been unfair but given the length of the relationship, I didn't think it justified him keeping any of my money. Yes, he owed me money, but the excuses become more and more ridiculous as time went on. I realised that money was not something that liked to hang around him. In fact, it seemed to run from him the way I ran from rodents. I had doubts that I would ever get my money back and started plotting ways to get even. He told me how his mom tried to control him by helping him with money and now I was doing the same thing. He then confessed that he didn't work all the time. That was the moment I realised that this man worked to weed and nothing else.

When he plays the creative card... chances are he's a crackhead

He told me that in order to complete his ten-year project, he needed to smoke weed. Apparently, creatives need drugs to create which suggests that we are all creative if we buy the right shit. We just don't know it yet. I found any sort of drug restricted my creativity and just made me jumpy and paranoid. Like we needed another suspicious black woman on the streets of London? I can't. But yeah, he stuck to this narrative.

When he loses a lot of weight... you're dating a crackhead

Thanks to Facebook you can track a weight loss. With the appropriate snooping, I could see that about a year before, he was big, but now, he was more than 100 lbs lighter. He had that loose skin that came from a dramatic weight loss that you see on *Biggest Loser*. I asked why and he told me that shit had got so hard despite being in a relationship that he lost weight from lack of food. The only other causes I know are illness and drugs. Food weight loss isn't usually that extreme in such a short period of time. Hell, we could all afford to skip the odd snack. I was disappointed that our breakup led to weight gain and not weight loss for me but I guess I didn't have medicinal help.

When he looks pained at the thought of spending money on anybody but himself... chances are he's a crackhead

Admittedly, he could be cheap but, no. When we went grocery shopping, I could see that the person didn't want to feed me. The worst was when the portion of rice he prepped was so small because he was trying to stretch out a packet of ready-made Uncle Ben's Wild Rice over three to four meals for two people. Another time was when the bill came and he gave me *that look* because I dared order a starter. Those were the most emotionally expensive ribs I'd ever order – at $18. Please note that this was the *only* meal he paid for in two visits. So basically, he was calculating how much money he had to spend on drugs by skimping on everything else.

There were plenty of other signs. The lateness that I put down to African time, the nervousness and anxiety, the waking up to finding him mindlessly finger-fucking me all zoned out, his inability to stay awake for calls or remember what time to call, the dry mouth, the night sweats as he detoxed... all signs that he was a crackhead.

Be warned.

American Dream – The Nightmare Ends

This wasn't me chasing a celebrity crush or a married man. This, my precious, is a tale of a woman owed and almost meeting Judge Mathis. Don't lend men money!

As I said, after the breakup dude still owed me money. It's a funny thing when you lend someone money thinking 'together forever' when really, they're just a wasteman and you happen to be the soft person that helps them pay those tricky things like cable and rent. I have to admit that I hate lending money, but I hate sitting in a flat and hearing the landlord knock on the door and phone for the rent even more. Yes, times were indeed hard. I learned a lot. Like when a man tells you they have a job you need to ask if it's full-time because six hours a week isn't cutting it. Elsewhere we call that volunteering or an internship. It shouldn't be my problem.

It was well-evidenced that the money was owed. I don't watch *Judge Judy* for the sake of my health. I had my emails, texts, Viber, etc. Yes, he wasn't clear on when he would pay me back, but the *asap* suggested that it would be *asap*. I've also learned that you have to chase and chase hard in writing. The longer you leave it, the less sympathy a judge will have for you. As an aside Judge Milian from *The People's Court* made a comment that she is constantly seeing women who have loaned money to men. It's a sickness of our times that we think is normal.

Then the excuses came. He had to wait for a refund. This is like the eternal, "I'll pay you from my taxes excuse." It means it's not going to happen. Then he had to put in an invoice. Another month he wasn't working at all so apparently that was my problem. I was clear – not my problem. That's the beauty of a breakup. He should have waited until he had the money to become a complete douche. You need to plan your 'arseholedness' people. Don't spring that shit on people when you're indebted.

Anyway, this dragged on for four whole months which was longer than the official relationship. My stress and frustration were increasing. So, I started to think... what if he refused to pay? Yes, I had my emails and texts saved but we were in separate countries and the laws were different. I started doing my research about foreign small claims. The judge could have argued that I couldn't get any travelling costs so would it be worth going to the US to get my money back?

Then I saw an episode of *Judge Mathis* and thought, yes, he could help me. He'd probably chew me out for loaning a man who I suspected of having a huge drug problem and no proper job money but, that was a risk I was willing to take. I thought about my evidence and that all important question: what would I wear? Chicago is a harsh place in the winter, so I'd have to push for a summer court date. Would I get to meet Doyle? All sorts of things ran through my head. Oh, and getting my money back.

And just when I was about ready to give up and had threatened him with a Mathis day in court... he paid me. My emails had started to make clar that I wasn't about to let this go. I had a whole social media plan B he didn't know about but may have guessed. Yes, he got the last kick in the teeth by doing it by PayPal e-cheque instead of directly but, I got my money or at least, I got it four days later when the cheque cleared.

Don't ever lend a man you're not married to any money in which case it's not a loan because you can't loan within a marriage. Another lesson learned from Judge Mathis. Thank you Judge!

And now I'm going to work on my addiction to court TV. It's going to be hard.

18. Finally

OK, so I was coming towards the end of my detox. I was eating better thanks to giving up chocolate for a year, although, to be fair, I had simply replaced it with Haribos. I was getting lots more exercise, as it became clear that stamina was essential for my sex drive and to feeling good about myself. I was closer to wanting to date again. All of the sex dating was fun for a while, but I didn't even make it to a year before I realised that this activity attracted even sadder individuals than traditional or internet dating. This wasn't the scene for me.

I had achieved something key though – a sense of my own sexuality and identity which had somehow been lost in seven years of being told that I was too much. Of course I'm too much. I do everything to excess and I have a fad approach to anything I do. I'm not an addict though my singirls, no need to worry.

So, it was to be expected that I wouldn't be every man's cup of chai. I was slowly learning though that whilst I was flexible in what I wanted in a man, I was certain that I wanted a man who would love me for me and not think

I was 'too' anything. Too is one of those words that turn something from a positive to a negative. She's too outgoing or she's too nice or she's too willing to compromise. OK nobody has ever accused me of these traits, but they have said that I'm too much or too particular or whatever it is that highlights their insecurity as opposed to my faults.

I realised that I was ready to traditionally date again. I was going to give the internet another try as it had the greatest options, but I was also going to ask people to hook me up. Not my mother, you understand, as she wasn't discriminating enough, but other people who would be able to help.

Little did I know that I was about to start dating properly again in a time when the whole world was entering a dating recession. But I was going to try. That's all I could do my singirls… try… as being a girl with a plan clearly wasn't working. I really hope you've enjoyed my dating tales but before I go, let me share some tips on two very important topics – how to handle that 'are you single' question and how to get ready for dating.

Still Single?

That perennially boring question and one that insults and pities at the same time. Yes, I'm still single thanks for asking. Until it changes and I take out a full ad in the *Metro* assume that things haven't changed. You see no ring on my finger and I'm not using the plural. Being single is fluid.

Can we stop asking this? Ask about my work (OK maybe not about my work) or ask about my holiday plans or ask about family, but don't ask about my sex status. It's annoying. I don't ask you how your mediocre marriage is going. I assume if things have changed and he's finally left you then, you would let us all know, right? So, here's how we tackle it my singirls.

Standard Responses

The other evening, I went to a networking group where I was asked this four times. Mainly by well-meaning friends. It's not a small talk question as the follow up is always a guess at why.

"Maybe you don't go out enough."

"You need to lower your standards."

"Is it because you aren't making enough effort?"

"Why don't you try Happn/Tinder/Bumble/eHarmony? I have a friend who did and now she's married with 16 chickens, two children and a puppy."

"Don't give up. I'm sure it will happen soon."

"It will happen when you least expect it!"

What's with all of these 'happenings' like not being single is a monumental event. I've not been single so many times. Almost as many times as I've been single. This is not landing on Venus folks. This is more slip and sliding on sweaty bodies until you get bored. Can we stop pretending it's the second coming of Tevin Campbell please?

What's the problem here?

What I slowly realised is that social media has killed the art of small talk as those who follow you think they know it all because you posted a few wasteman rants. That said we still think women's worth should be measured by her marital status. I asked one of the guys if his single status was ever questioned and he laughed at me as he replied, "Of course not, I'm a guy."

The ones that piss me off the most are the smugly new couples. You've only just got a double bed and yet you're behaving as if you've worked out a scientific cure for singledom. No, you met someone and now you're less single. Let's keep it real. He's three hissy fits and a call from his ex away and you're always on the lookout for an upgrade. So, let's not chat shit. You can never afford to be smug in this modern age.

I wish them all a #stayblessed as I continue to fill my days up with things that I want to do, not things that I'm supposed to do in the vain hopes of 'catching' a man. But the next time you finding yourself asking that question take a moment and think, why am I asking that when we could be talking about food?

Why I (sometimes) date younger men

Life is wonderful. You are constantly out, the champagne is flowing and your life is being carefully documented through Facebook photo albums. It limits the number of times you can wear the same outfit but apart from that all is well. I was very clear that I dated men that were older and had the weight and gravitas to ensure that I could always afford my black cab fetish.

Then you start to realise that there are fewer people to go out with. Couples complain it's too cold or have travel plans, friends are all pregnant and finally you are the last party starter left in the bar. Party for one is not a phrase that is likely to catch on. It used to be that you would take your fabulousness to the gay bars of Soho but alas, these too are emptier of people your own age as marriage and adoption are more common. And Vauxhall is too far and too testosterone fuelled. I would like to personally thank Elton John for the misery that is my social life.

So with the options limited and the dating pool shrinking at an alarming rate, I realised....I had to do something. Not only did I need someone to plus one all the weddings I'm constantly invited to but I have other needs that need to be met to avoid me killing tourists on the left hand side of the escalator. So here are my weak reasons for rethinking my views on dating younger men.

Stamina

We all know that age and sexual peak are related. Furthermore, with the internet there isn't that big an experience gap as once was. Some of these young'uns didn't have to sneak that one porn tape into their house to learn what sex was all about. I like knowing that round 2 and 3 aren't dreams. And they are keen enough to learn and be guided.

Baggage

Yes you will have to listen to tales of scuffed trainers, T-shirts and group dynamics of people whose names you don't care to remember but there is a carefree energy the young have that make them attractive. And they still believe they could make it big bless 'em. This is the age to date wannabe rappers. Don't wait until they're in their 30s and them jumping around the stage with that middle age spread just looks like an uncle at the wrong wedding. Get the dreamers with true potential who don't yet have the emotional and physical baggage to be bitter. But be careful! Too young and he may still be battling puppy fat. It's a thin line my precious.

Fun

Maybe it's because you don't go into it wondering if this is potentially the father of your children. There is something more fun about spending time with someone who isn't talking about mortgages, redundancy and pensions. Their only stress is handing in an assignment or getting to work from yours on time but that's about it. Probably because their mum still does their washing and cooking. Maybe dating them is just a reminder to you of your younger more confident self. It helps you get a piece of that joie de vivre back. And normally they can still laugh at themselves. But only just. Be careful not to tease them too much as they do have a tendency to sulk.

Learning to use apps / social media /chat

I was well proud of myself for reaching double figures on my Whatsapp contacts. I had finally arrived! I have 12 conversations going and even a group chat. Then I met a younger guy who was juggling 200. I had one boyfriend whose mobile number I never even knew. All arrangements and meetings were handled by our Facebook messenger. I have however learned that one inappropriate emoticon cannot be fixed with three others and a plea to ignore the previous messages. Apparently, what you say on messenger counts as the sort of thing you can't take back.

So, ladies let's not dismiss the 20 – 28 year olds. They may not be ready for everything you have planned but they have much better bodies. And there is nothing wrong with building a new dating pool if the old one starts to get dry.

Dating Readiness

I'm often told that relationships are about compromise but when it comes to dating, we women often do ourselves a disservice by not being prepared.

Yes, I know you've just blown £300 getting everything waxed, polished and redone for the big date. But, if like me you're coming out of a relationship where you compromised then it's worth taking the time to figure out what it is that you really want. And let's stop compromising during the dating stage. There's plenty of time for that in marriage and living together, trust me.

Put you first

He calls and asks for a date. You have a deadline but find yourself agreeing as he convinces you that this is the only time he can squeeze you in. One guy always had to work late; he did accounting not lifesaving work. So eventually I made alternative plans and only met him when it suited me. He rang and I told him I already had a date. It was a stay-at-home rom com marathon and snacks. Solo dates are just as important.

Equally, I realised that my exes all maintained their Sunday football or *Star Trek* obsessions, but I would deny myself my Saturday shopping spree. or concert tour or a lazy read just to spend quality time with him and his problems. After a breakup, their social lives went on seamlessly but mine... well there is only so much shopping and socialising my bank manager would allow me to do. But now I'm precious about my time and my hobbies. They're what keep me sane.

Be Safe

I've taken some unnecessary risks on this journey and I regret being nice where sometimes I should have just been brutal and saved myself the ensemble and calories. It's never wrong to say, nope, not feeling this and walking out.

Know your deal breakers and values

When he told me to 'shh' during sex and said that his mum was asleep in the other room, I realised that men who still lived in their mum's house with no plans of moving were a deal breaker for me. PAYG is my other one. Commit to a contract brother.

I've also learned about my values. One guy I met didn't eat pork. I spent a day searching for non-pork sausages for breakfast. But then as I looked lingeringly at the bacon aisle, I realised that a man that couldn't enjoy one of my famous fry ups wasn't a match. I respected this value of his, but it wasn't one I could share.

173

Only date the attractive

I'm tired of being told that what I want doesn't exist or good luck finding it. I've dated every type of guy to show that I'm open. Like, why was I talking to the tall Swede who clearly only wanted to culturally explore? Or the player with wandering eyes? I've learned that dating means having faith that what you need exists.

But my instincts have never steered me wrong. So now I only date those I immediately find attractive or connect with. This isn't *CSI: Crime Scene Investigation*. I can't forensically dissect every date in the hopes of finding the clue to what may make us a great couple. I stick to what my heart wants which right now is hot chocolate.

Ask yourself if you're really ready

It's ok not to be dating ready. Sometimes you have other things to do or you want to explore your interests. Don't be pressured into thinking that dating is something you have to do constantly. It's tiring. Take those union breaks and replenish your energies. Being vulnerable and cute isn't an easy look to pull off.

If you're not in a dating space then that's ok too. Just be clear when you're asked out that you're not in that space and move on. If they're worth the effort then trust me, they'll still be around when you are ready. After all, that's why the friend zone is really there.

I wish you all the best on your dating misadventures.

Happy dating!

Thank You

My parents for telling everyone I was a writer way before I dared call myself one – partly to avoid telling people they weren't sure what I did.

Alan Jay who told me to write more content every day when I was congratulating myself on merely writing.

Conscious Dreams Publishing Founder Danni Blechner and Editor Rhoda Molife for their tireless back and forthing and encouragement throughout this process.

To my friends for their constant feedback and dialogue even if that was silence – Samantha.

To my Facebook and Twitter families – just because you are virtual doesn't make you less valuable.

Mrs Lewis, my English teacher who gave me a good mark for an essay that I thought was rather awful.

Sister Magdalene who made me fall in love with language and Latin. One day I will visit Pompeii.

My favourite lecturers at Wits: Ann Smith and Karen Lazar, who taught me that feminism isn't a dirty word.

All the men I've dated, almost dated, slept with, almost married, crushed over. You rock and forgive me if I didn't tell everyone how amazing you truly are but your screw ups were far more fun to write about. Some of you sucked. Your insecurities, baggage and behaviour have made women realise it's not us… most of the time you're right when you say that it's you!

I'm out of here. I probably have a date or something to go on, write about or plan. Or maybe I'll just chat nonsense online and see what comes up. Love you all!

Chelsea Black 2020

About the Author

Chelsea Black is a writer, consultant and radio host who currently lives in London. Her dating journey has been featured in *The Voice* newspaper and on *Singles Warehouse*. Her blog, *Chelsea Black*, has been selected for the Vuelio Top 10 Dating and Relationship Blogs twice. She is a lover of romance movies and has a lifelong relationship with chocolate and sweets. She is allergic to the gym.

Conscious Dreams
PUBLISHING

Be the author of your own destiny

Find out about our authors, events, services
and how you too can get your book journey started.

 Conscious Dreams Publishing

 @DreamsConscious

 @consciousdreamspublishing

 Daniella Blechner

 www.consciousdreamspublishing.com

 info@consciousdreamspublishing.com

Let's connect

Lightning Source UK Ltd.
Milton Keynes UK
UKHW021349230221
379252UK00011BB/365